For all the young people who have taught us so much about anxiety, their honesty and courage.

For Maureen; her compassion, strength and unreasonably messy desk will not be forgotten.

CONTENTS

Acknowledgements

We each have our own family, friends and mentors whose support we have valued and appreciated and without whom we might never have written this book. They have not only shared their own thoughts and experiences, but also most importantly have helped us to manage (and forget) our own anxieties and doubts about writing down our personal and professional ideas about dealing with anxiety. We hope you know who you are.

In special thanks, Phoebe would like to say a big and extra special thank you to her parents without whom she could not have come so far in overcoming her anxieties and would not feel so able to talk about her anxiety as she has in this book. Sue would like to say a huge thank you to her partner Ben for all his support, and her beautiful sons; the eldest of whom has been paid in ice-cream for his thoughts on each chapter. Bridie would like to thank her partner Chris for his encouragement and support, and their energetic children for keeping her so busy she no longer has time to worry about anything.

We are so grateful to every family and young person who has shared their hurts, worries, failures and successes, both in this book and in our work. You have inspired us and taught us so much about anxiety, coping and resilience.

For those of you who have been brave enough to share your stories here, we think you are amazing, and it would not have been the book we hoped for without you.

Many thanks to our draft readers (Steve, Andy and Tom) for your feedback, patience and attention to detail. Finally, thank you to Kim, Amy, Steve, Emily and the team at JKP for agreeing with us that this book was a good idea and helping us get it out to as many young people who are dealing with anxiety as possible.

Preface

There are several reasons why we decided to write this book. We know how common anxiety is for young people and how difficult it can be to get help. We also know that different things work for different people (no one is the same), so we have tried to include lots of different techniques and strategies, so that you can see what works best for you. This book belongs to YOU (as long as you haven't borrowed it from the library!) so feel free to highlight, underline and add post-its in when you are reading through and see bits that fit with you. Then, at the end of the book, you can put all these bits together in your Anxiety Survival Plan.

We wanted this book to echo our belief that anxiety is a normal, healthy, human emotion – but sometimes it can become so big that it can get in the way of everyday life. There are lots of quotes and personal experiences throughout the book, and Chapter 12 has young people's stories about their anxieties, worries and learning to cope, which we hope you will find useful.

Whilst writing this book, we were very aware that we continue to experience our own anxieties. Recently, Bridie panicked after thinking that she had accidentally saved over Sue's chapter; Sue had been anxiously waiting for an email reply from the publisher and jumping every time her phone beeped; and Phoebe was restless with apprehension and excitement – she had never helped to write a book before!

We hope that you find this book useful and we wish you all the best in your journey getting back on track.

Sue, Bridie and Phoebe

x

❧ 1 ❧

Anxiety - The Basics

What exactly is anxiety?

Anxiety is what happens when our bodies think we are under threat. It's a feeling that most people describe as unpleasant, but the physical sensations can actually be very similar to feelings of excitement. The difference when we're anxious is that we also have anxious thoughts or interpret the feeling as "bad". Other words that are commonly used to describe feeling anxious are "nervous", "fearful" or "worried".

Everyone responds a little differently when they are anxious. Some people feel anxiety mostly in their body with sensations in their stomach, chest and even sometimes in their arms and legs. Other people might say that anxiety is "in their head" because the main thing they notice is that their thoughts go very fast. These things happen in our body and our mind because when our body notices a "threat", it responds in the way that it has since we were living in caves. Back then, we were threatened by predators and worried about being clubbed to death by other cavemen. Now, we might be more worried about exams and feel threatened by new groups of people. So, in the way that it has for eons, your brain uses the information collected by your eyes and ears to detect threats in your environment and, without consulting you, releases a number of chemicals that have immediate effects on both your body and the way that you think.

These chemicals affect your breathing, your digestion, heart rate, blood flow and muscle tension. The aim is to make you ready to get very far away from the threat quickly (*flight*), kick the hell out of that caveman (*fight*) or pretend you are dead so he goes away and leaves you alone (*freeze*). So, your heart rate and breathing speed up, your blood flows away from your internal organs and towards your arms and legs so they are ready for running or fighting and your muscles tense up ready to go. The unintended consequences can be that you feel tense and a bit sick, or get butterflies in your stomach. You could start to sweat and feel light-headed or a bit dizzy, even though you might be sitting still. All these reactions are super clever ways of your brain helping you to be ready and prepared to manage threat. However, as threats have changed significantly since this threat system evolved, these reactions are not as useful as they once were. If we don't understand what our body is doing, then these reactions and the "symptoms" themselves can cause even more anxiety.

Some people experience anxieties every day; other people only feel anxious occasionally. Some people's brains will kick off the chemical reactions much more easily than others. We think, from looking at the research, that this can be because they were either born with a sensitive threat system (genes) or because they have had more difficult and stressful experiences (environment) or both. We talk about this in more detail in Chapter 2. There are lots of individual differences, but what we know is that *everyone* experiences anxiety.

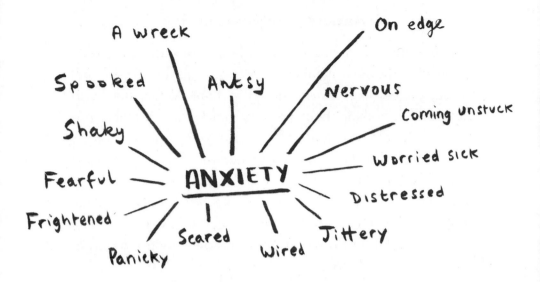

What happens when I'm anxious?

Anxious thoughts

When we are anxious, several things happen to the way we think. It becomes easier to think of negative rather than positive outcomes, we get stuck on "what if" questions, and our thinking brain shuts down and our threat brain (focused solely on survival) takes over. This means that we struggle to use the bits of our brains that usually would help us to solve problems and see the wider context, because these bits are offline whilst we manage the threat. Our anxious brains choose between "flight", "fight" or "freeze" rather than from the full range of behaviours or responses that are usually available to us. This is a really effective way of dealing with physical threats that were common for cavemen, but it does not serve us so well in complex social situations that we find ourselves in now.

Anxious bodily sensations

Some of the sensations in the body that anxiety can create have already been mentioned. We can get butterflies, feel tense, or feel like we are going to faint. When the heart rate and breathing become very quick and thoughts are racing, people sometimes think that they are going to pass out, die or that they are losing control. Everyone feels a little different when they are anxious, but the main thing to remember is that these sensations are *normal* and healthy. Although they feel horrible, they are not in any way harmful to us. They are just a bit outdated in how they are trying to protect us from threats.

Nausea

Shaking

Racing heart

Sweating

Anxious behaviours

The most common behaviour that we see when people are anxious is that they *avoid* the thing that they think is making them anxious. They might even avoid places where they think it is more likely that they will feel anxious or where they think the trigger (the cause or source) for the anxiety might be. If we feel that we can't get away from the trigger for our anxiety, we might raise our voices and/or become more animated, or, otherwise, we might become extremely quiet and still. We can go back to the evolution of anxiety and the flight, fight, freeze responses to understand these behaviours. The problem with avoidance as our "go to" behaviour when we are anxious is that we never get to test out whether we really needed to be anxious about that situation in the first place or whether we can cope when things do get difficult. For example, a teacher asks you a question in class, not a particularly difficult question, but because you weren't paying full attention, your mind goes blank. You feel everyone waiting and looking at you, so you start to feel very self-conscious; you flush red, your palms are sweating, and your heart is beating out of your chest. After a few seconds (that feels like much longer) the teacher moves on to one of your classmates who answers the question correctly. Following this experience, just the thought of a teacher asking you a question makes you feel anxious and your heart beat faster. You start to do small things to become less visible in class, for example not making eye contact with your teachers, so that no one picks you in class. You stop volunteering answers entirely. In the short term, this makes you feel safer ("Phew, no teachers picked me today") but, in the long term, you are less involved in the class, you stop getting positive feedback from your teachers and you lose opportunities to learn that you *can* answer questions and even cope with awkward silences. If you continue to avoid answering questions in class and feel like you just cannot do it, then this story about you being "incapable" becomes a "fact" and you have a really big problem.

What is great about anxiety?

You might think this is a very silly section of the chapter, especially if anxiety is currently making your life miserable. However, it is important to remember that anxiety is useful and we wouldn't want to be without it. We developed flight, fight and freeze for a very good reason and although we now have more complex worries and things to be scared of, we still need our anxiety to make our lives work.

Imagine if parents didn't feel anxious about their new baby? Dads might not bother to baby-proof the house, mums might not bother to check that the car seats are attached properly. None of these things work out very well for the baby.

Worrying about exams might be stressful, but is it worse than not worrying about exams? If we didn't have any anxiety about the future, then we would probably just sit and eat ice-cream rather than revising. After all, which is more fun and pleasant?

In this book, we do not aim to rid you of anxiety. This might sound like a blissful idea, but we really think that your anxiety is an important and useful part of your life. It might just need some understanding, and maybe some taming, to make sure it is helping more than it is causing you problems.

What is an anxiety disorder?

There's a lot more discussion and information about "mental health disorders" around now. This can sound a bit scary! When we talk about "anxiety disorders", all it really means is when anxiety starts to interfere with school, friendships and your daily activities. It also means that your anxiety has been around for longer than a few days or even weeks, but has stuck around for months.

There are some disagreements between psychologists and other mental health professionals about diagnosis and the use of the word "disorder". Some people think that it's a useful, non-blaming way to help people to understand the way feelings and behaviours can become problematic; others think it makes people feel that there is something wrong with them for being distressed. One of the main arguments against using the word "disorder" is that suffering and distress are part of being human, so why do we treat it like illness?

We (the people writing this book) think the most important thing to remember is that anxiety is normal, but that we should not ignore distress. It is really important that you don't try to "manage" anxiety like an illness if there is a clear cause. Often feeling anxious is your body and brain's way of telling you that there is something wrong in your environment and that you, or the adults around you, need to make a change. For example, if someone is hurting or humiliating you and this is making you feel anxious, you should not work on the anxiety but on the cause instead. We know that it can feel really scary telling someone about what is happening because you are worried that they won't believe you, or might blame you for what is happening. This is rarely the case. We can assure you that letting a trusted adult know (whether this is a parent, teacher or someone else that you feel safe with) means that they can help to make it stop, support you or give you advice about what to do next. If someone is hurting you and you don't feel that there is anyone you can talk to about it, there are organisations that you can contact who can help and advise you (see Useful Information section at the end of the book).

In Chapter 11 we say a bit more about how to tell someone you are feeling anxious.

Who gets a diagnosis of anxiety disorder?

Sometimes the term "anxiety disorder" is written down by a professional and then it becomes something that you "have". It's OK to question professionals about how they have come to these decisions. Other times you might be told exactly what is happening and go through a structured process of answering lots of questions about your anxiety and how it affects your life. A diagnosis should only be given if anxiety has been around for a number of months and causes significant problems at home and school, and/or in your social life. The impact of anxiety should be assessed from your perspective and from the perspective of those who know you best such as parents and teachers.

Diagnoses are often used to help the professionals decide on the best way to help you with the problem and to begin to develop a shared understanding.

Formulation is another way of understanding anxiety. The difference from diagnosis is that it uses a story about your fears, worries or behaviours instead of a label. A story means that it is more personal to you and includes your needs and strengths. Formulation also thinks about how past experiences may have impacted upon the anxiety that you feel now, and the ways that you cope with it (see Chapter 2 for more information about where anxiety comes from). Formulation aims to identify what is keeping your anxiety going so you can take steps to get back on track. The Anxiety Survival Plan in Chapter 13 should get you started on making your own formulation.

Will problem anxiety go away on its own?

We know that about 1 in 20 young people will experience anxiety so severe that it could be considered a "disorder". We also know that most of them will recover and no longer suffer from anxiety that causes them severe problems by the time they reach adulthood. So, you could just hope that you get through a tough time and it goes away because for most people it does. However, we also know that most adults who suffer with severe anxiety started to struggle with anxiety when they were a child or adolescent. We think it's really helpful if young people develop an understanding of anxiety early in their life and find the coping skills and strategies for managing anxiety that suit them. If you master these skills now, then you are ready for anything! You can read about young people who have suffered with anxiety and found their way through it in Chapter 12. We also know that at some point it becomes a significant problem for about 1 in 10 adults. Your understanding and skills will mean that you are well equipped both for everyday stresses and if life throws something really stressful at you.

How does this book help with anxiety?

In this book, we aim to provide you with information and young people's stories that will help you to better understand your anxiety and where it might come from, and to explain a number of different approaches and strategies to help you to feel more in control of your anxiety. The ideas that we have included come from research studies, our experiences of working with young people, and the experiences of young people like Phoebe and what they have found most helpful. You will probably find some of the approaches helpful and others not so much; we think that's OK as what works best for one person might not work so well for the next. It is also important to remember that we need different strategies at different times, so keep an open mind. We hope that you can try out some of these ideas and put together your own personalised Survival Plan (see Chapter 13), which you can share with people whom you are close to, to help you feel in control of your anxiety and able to face anything.

❧ 2 ❧

Understanding Where My Anxiety Comes From

If you are really struggling with your anxiety, you might be thinking, "Why me?!" When we look around at our friends, teachers and even our families, it might seem like we are the only ones who are struggling with these feelings of fear or nervousness, and the only people whose lives are limited by them. We know from research that you are definitely not alone. Anxiety affects the lives of many people each year, both young and old – so why does it often feel so isolating?

In many modern cultures we teach our children not to show weaknesses or sore spots to others. Lots of us have learned from school, or from our parents, that when we feel negative emotions such as anxiety or sadness, we should hide it and "put on a brave face" so that we don't "look like a baby" and are seen to be "acting our age". We learn that it is OK to show fear when we are little, but we are taught that this is something that is not acceptable to show to other people when we are grown up. In many cultures this is particularly true for boys and young men, but we can all feel the pressure to be seen to be coping, or even thriving, all of the time. Now that everyone uses social media to represent their lives to others, there is even more pressure to be seen to be successful and happy all the time.

Sometimes it is helpful to use a brave face to get through difficult or scary situations, as we learn from this experience that actually it isn't as bad as we thought and we can manage the anxiety more easily than we had anticipated; this is called "Fake it 'till you make it". However, sometimes, when we feel that it is unacceptable to show a part of ourselves or our true feelings to others, we then hide our fears. We end up feeling totally alone with these awful feelings and then they often get a greater grip on us and the choices that we make in the future.

There are lots of reasons why you might be feeling more anxious than the people around you at this point in your life (although it is important to remember that other people might just be better at hiding their fears!).

WHAT CONTRIBUTES TO WHY YOUNG PEOPLE SUFFER WITH ANXIETY?

☆ the way we are made – biology or genes

☆ our individual temperament – including how we react to new or scary stuff

☆ our very early experiences of being cared for

☆ parents' or carers' fears and behaviours

☆ traumatic or scary experiences

☆ bereavement – losing people we love

☆ transitions – having lots of major changes in our lives

☆ stressors – pressure and stress in the environment.

Biology

We know that some babies are more sensitive than others and have different responses to new sensations and experiences. Psychologists would say these babies have an "anxious temperament" as they are more easily upset than other babies at something new and then take a bit longer to calm down. We know that some of the differences in babies is due to the combination of genes that they inherited from their parents. Some come from the environment in the mother's womb and yet more come from the early environment once the baby is born and how this affects the genes. It is most definitely complicated and we won't go on about it too much. The environment and people around you when you are a baby affect the way that your brain biology develops, which affects your bodily sensations and how you interpret new things that happen in the world. No one gene or factor decides whether we will be more anxious than others or not. It depends how lots of things come together to impact the complex person who is unique you. It just seems that some inherited genes make you more sensitive to new things, and make anxious bodily responses more likely. These things can put someone at greater risk for problem anxiety.

Biology does not explain everything; it might be that you did well in the gene lottery, but life has simply thrown more stresses at you than you have ways or resources to cope with. If you are usually a calm and easy-going person who rarely experiences anxiety, you can still experience times of high stress and your threat brain then quickly becomes more active and sensitive. Everyone has times in their life when they feel like they are "going under" and this is OK. *It's OK to not be OK*. If you are used to being a "coper", then these stressful times, and feeling that you are not managing, can be a big shock and make you question some of your ideas about yourself. This challenge to how you think about yourself can be even more unsettling and stressful.

We know that we cannot do much to change the genes that we inherited; however, we like to remind ourselves and the young people whom we work with that the genes that make us more prone to anxiety can also be a good thing. Being sensitive and responsive are great qualities that have many benefits for you and those close to you; it just means that you might have to take more time to learn about and understand your bodily sensations and your thoughts, so you can find ways to manage them effectively and feel more in control.

Early experiences

Although we often don't remember the things that happen to us when we are very little, they can still have important and lasting effects on our brains and how we feel about ourselves, others and the world around us. We know that if life was tough for us and our parents when we were babies, this can have a lasting impact on how we grow and develop. Just like our genes, we can't do much to change this; however, it can be extremely important to acknowledge that even if it feels as though our fears and worries "come from nowhere", they do come from our experience, even if we don't remember it. Usually difficulties with anxiety can be understood by looking at our current environment and/or the difficult things that happened when we were little. If things were hard when we were little, this can have an impact on important relationships, like those with our parents or caregivers. It can make it hard to trust others, which means when life gets stressful it is hard to reach out. We know from research that the best way for people to manage stress is to have a trusted person close to them.

You might not know much about your early life and maybe you don't wish to right now. It can be hard to think about difficult times and it's not always necessary to understand exactly why we feel the way we do to find effective ways to manage anxiety. However, if you are finding it very hard to trust others and this has always been a problem for you, it might be worth talking to a professional about these issues to try to build your trust and ability to relate to other people so that they can help you when times are tough. There are lots of people who might be or become your trusted other or adult. It might be a parent or carer, or it could be a teacher or school counsellor. Many people will have an aunt, uncle or sibling whom they feel more able to turn to for comfort and advice. Having someone who gets you and your anxiety can really make the difference.

Parents' and carers' behaviours

Parents usually want the very best for their children and will try to protect them from hearing, seeing or experiencing anything bad. Lots of parents are aware that their own fears and worries can be passed on to their children and so try to hide them around their children. However, as you probably already know, hiding fears and worries from those close to you is not always easy and is sometimes plain impossible. We can learn anxious beliefs, for example, "Spiders are evil!" or anxious behaviours, for example, "Run run run!" from listening to and watching our parents when they are scared.

A less obvious example might be if your mum and/or dad are nervous around other people and worry about what they think. This may mean that they spent less time socialising with others when you were little, so you didn't develop confidence in being around lots of people. Parents might also have said things like, "What will [friend or neighbour]

think of our scruffy garden/my terrible haircut?" Over time, these worries can give children important messages about the world and other people that they might have taken on without realising it. Parents often feel very bad or sad about their children worrying about the same things that have made them miserable; we don't want to make parents feel any worse. We think it can be important to think about how you developed your fears and worries so that you can start to question where some of your ideas about what is scary might have come from. Then you can decide whether you think they are (a) true and (b) helpful. Lots of children are aware of their parents' fears and anxieties, but have never discussed the issue directly with them. We know that children with an anxious temperament are more likely to worry and pick up anxious messages from parents. Anxious children can see tiny cues about fear and anxiety that other children don't notice.

As we mentioned in Chapter 1, avoidance of things that make us feel anxious is a useful and normal human response. However, we can learn from those around us that this is the best (or even the only) way to cope when we feel under threat. When people who are close to us feel scared about facing fears, then it can make it much harder for us to be brave and try new ways to approach the source of fear and anxiety.

Traumatic or scary experiences

Sadly, sometimes really scary and horrible things happen to people. They might live with someone who is unpredictable or aggressive, or their family might have lived somewhere unsafe and scary. Parents can't always protect their children in the way that they might like and some parents can't keep their children safe at all. For other young people, they may have had relatively safe and happy lives, but something like a car accident or a crime might have suddenly made them feel terrified and uncertain about the world.

Once you are removed from the unsafe environment, or the traumatic event is over, then you and the people around you might expect that you will feel OK again. Our brains and bodies, however, take some time to make sense of and move on from these events and experiences. Sometimes, you might need quite a lot of help to feel safe again as your threat system and anxious thoughts, bodily sensations, and behaviours will be in overdrive. Following a difficult experience, it is likely that your very sensitive threat system can see threats where no threat really exists. We call these "false alarms". A sensitive threat system is common to all kinds of anxiety, but after a traumatic event false alarms are normal and to be expected for a few weeks. It is only if this carries on for a number of months that we would think about this as a problem or something that should lead to someone seeking support. Lots of the strategies that we talk about in this book will be useful for people who are experiencing difficult anxiety reactions following trauma. However, this book does not deal specifically with the results of trauma, which can sometimes require different interventions to be effective.

It is important to acknowledge that our experiences and environments will have impacted on our level of, and responses to, anxiety. Most important, however, is that if you are still living in a scary and unsafe environment, or things are happening to you that you feel upset or uncomfortable about, then we would not want you to focus solely on managing your anxiety, but rather, we would want you to seek support to end the situation that is causing you so much stress (see Useful Information section at the end of the book). For example, in Leon's story (see Chapter 12), he talks about how he experienced bullying at school that was making him feel anxious. For him to start to feel better, he needed support from other people to end the bullying (rather than just coping with how it was making him feel).

Loss and bereavement

When someone dies, parents separate, or a friend moves away, we can feel a lot of different difficult emotions. Losing someone we love is one of the most painful things that a human being can experience. The most common and overwhelming emotion is often sadness; however, anger, confusion, numbness and anxiety are also common experiences following losses too. Even if we have been lucky and felt safe for most of our life, a bereavement can make us feel very fragile or vulnerable and suddenly threats seem to be everywhere. We may start to fear losing other important people and worry that we can't be sure that others will be around for us. If we have had a lot of difficult experiences and losses, then another bereavement can feel like it is the final straw that we just don't have the strength to cope with, triggering a lot of anxiety. If we worry about other people sticking around for us, we can become more isolated and feel that it is better to just depend on ourselves. This is understandable, but also a problem, because at these times we need other people even more to help us through them. Sadly, just like our early experiences, we cannot reverse losses, and relationships cannot always be mended. However, we think it is important to acknowledge how these experiences of losing important people and relationships affect how we think and feel about ourselves and other people, because this has a significant impact on our threat system, our level of anxiety and the resources that we have to help us cope with it.

Transitions

In Chapter 10, we talk in a lot more detail about the impact of big changes in our lives and how you can manage transitions effectively. Transitions can be exciting; however, change can also provoke a lot of anxiety, whether it is moving schools, a new teacher, or a big loss. It is important to acknowledge how change impacts on our wellbeing and levels of stress and anxiety. For some people, just changing classes at school or a disruption to routine can cause lots of stress, so the impact of transitions on our anxiety can be an important consideration. We know from working with young people that lots of transitions can mean lots of stress, and going through lots of transitions in your early life can lead to you being more anxious than young people who have had more stability in their environment and relationships.

Everyday pressures and stresses

Adolescence is a time where expectations change and you become increasingly independent. School expect that you demonstrate your learning through coursework and exams (see Chapter 9 for more information on coping with these) and these lead to independent new roles at work or university. Parents often expect you to demonstrate increasing responsibility, for example, taking on more chores or looking after pets and siblings. You might even end up caring for a parent who is sick or has their own mental health problems so you might be seen as more like an adult. If you feel ready and have developed ways to cope with stress, then these challenges can be extremely positive and lead to growth.

For some people, however, this pressure can cause a great deal of discomfort and distress. This can mean that the person just hasn't worked out what they need to do to feel OK when change or stress is around. Their coping skills are overloaded by the expectations of those around them. Once we think "I can't cope" we can get stuck in a vicious cycle; our beliefs about our ability to cope are just as important as our actual skills and abilities.

Bringing it all together

Sorry to say, we can't tell you exactly where your anxiety came from. We have outlined in this chapter that there are lots of different things that can lead to a person feeling anxious. Some people feel that everyday stresses are very difficult to cope with. Others feel that they are "copers" but then suddenly find themselves feeling extremely anxious. Some of the things that have contributed to our anxiety we can't even remember (like early experiences) and others we are not able to change (like the combination of genes we were born with).

One of the most important messages we want to get across is that one experience does not usually cause problematic anxiety. It is a complicated process that can involve our genes, early experiences, the behaviour of our parents, trauma and/or loss, and the amount of stress we are dealing with at any given time. We would also like you to remember that comparisons to other people are not helpful;

others might appear calm and confident, when they are actually feeling unsure and anxious underneath.

One final important thing we want to be clear about is that we think questioning and trying to understand where our beliefs and anxieties might come from can be a helpful thing to do. However, it isn't always necessary to fully understand what has caused it in order to make changes that make anxiety feel more manageable. Often, to really understand where anxieties come from, we need the help of a person we trust who can help us to build our understanding and this can be a good friend, a parent, or a counsellor/therapist.

❧ 3 ❧

Tackling Anxiety Head On

Avoiding Avoidance

One of the ways to tackle anxiety is to start to make changes to what we do and how we think about anxiety, in order to change the way we feel. Some readers might have heard of cognitive behavioural therapy, or CBT, as a treatment for anxiety. Cognitive is a word that we use to describe thoughts and thinking, so when people talk about CBT they are basically talking about making changes to the way we think and the way that we behave. The following chapters will describe ways to tackle anxiety by changing how we think when we are anxious, and by tackling worry. In this chapter, we will think about how these "head on" approaches work and what might get in the way, then move on to thinking about how we change our behaviour and stop avoidance keeping us in the anxious cycle.

Why take a cognitive behavioural approach?

So, why do we think you knowing how to use CBT to tackle your anxiety is a good idea? Well, first, we know that CBT is an effective treatment for around 60 per cent of children and young people who are suffering from an anxiety disorder. Tackling thoughts and behaviour to manage and reduce anxiety has been extensively researched, and the results show that it can reduce young people's anxiety. We also know from our own experiences of working with young people struggling with anxiety, and from managing our own fears and worries, that these techniques can be helpful and make us feel more in control.

Thoughts, feelings and behaviour

We have talked a little in Chapter 1 about how anxiety affects our thoughts and our behaviour. Now we can think a little bit about how our bodily sensations, thoughts and behaviour affect each other. Imagine you are at a friend's birthday party and someone that you know pushes past you, standing on your foot and spilling a drink down your new clothes.

What are you thinking? How do you feel and what is happening in your body? What might you do?

You might think, "How very rude!" or, "What a horrible thing to do" and feel either angry or hurt and upset. Your heart rate will probably start to go up and your breathing may get quicker. You might say something to the person to let them know they upset you or alternatively you might leave the party right away feeling awful.

Now imagine the same situation. You are at a friend's party and someone you know pushes past you, stands on your foot and spills a drink on your new clothes. However, this time you see that they are pale and sweaty and look rather unwell.

What are you thinking? How do you feel and what is happening in your body? What might you do?

You might think, "Oh dear, I hope they're OK" and you might feel concerned about that person with no real change in your body; your heart rate and breathing might stay the same (unless you feel very worried and think they are seriously ill). You are more likely to go and ask them if they are OK than tell them that they are rude. Probably in this situation, we are less likely to take it personally or want to leave.

What we think and how we make sense of a situation has a huge impact on our bodies' responses and our emotions, as well as what we are likely to do. In the first example, we saw a threat, so our response is flight, fight or freeze. In the second example, we are not feeling threatened so we can use a different part of our brain to see the wider context and then we can feel empathy for the other person.

It is important to remember that how we think, how we act and how we feel all impact on each other. So, if our bodies are already feeling anxious (perhaps because we don't really like parties), we are also more likely to interpret the situation as threatening. When we are anxious, our thinking is more focused on threats, so we might miss the signs that someone is unwell and jump to the conclusion that they did it to make us feel bad or because they think we are not important.

Vicious circles

In the situation above, we can see how vicious circles of anxious thoughts, bodily sensations and behaviours can quickly develop and make us feel more anxious and likely to avoid these situations in the future. If we choose to get out of the anxious situation, we could miss important information that might have changed how we perceived that situation. We may never learn that even if the worst-case scenario occurred, we could cope with it. The avoidance on that occasion can lead to thoughts like, "I can't cope with other people" and, "Those anxious feelings would have overwhelmed me" that kick off more anxious bodily sensations and make avoidance more likely. If we repeatedly avoid, then we never get to learn that the situation (e.g. going to the party) was not as awful as we had thought and that even if someone was horrible to us, although it wouldn't be great, we could cope with it OK. Avoidance can lead us to trust and believe our anxious thoughts and this will influence our behaviour the next time we are in that situation, or even a similar situation.

Breaking the cycle

One way that we can tackle anxiety head on is to do things that change the way our body is responding to anxiety. Relaxation exercises help us to slow down our breathing and to release the tension from our muscles. Chapter 7 talks in a lot of detail about different ways to help your body relax and then soothe the threat system when you are feeling anxious, so we won't talk any more about that in this chapter. Instead we will think first about how we can stop using avoidance to cope with scary situations.

Breaking the cycle by avoiding avoidance

Many anxious people are stuck in "flight" mode. It is one of the most efficient ways to avoid the horrible physical feelings that come with you perceiving threat when your body kicks in with its evolutionary system for handling danger. Getting far away from the sabre tooth tiger was often the most efficient and effective way of managing the threat and the most likely to lead to success (staying alive to eat more woolly mammoths and make caveman babies). As highly social beings who rely on other humans in many ways, fighting with each other every time we feel stressed out and uncomfortable would not really work in our favour.

Although everyone can lose it sometimes when they are backed into a corner and feel scared, the most common response is to get out of there fast. It works. We think this is a good place to start tackling your anxiety because:

- when you break the cycle and behave differently, this quickly has positive impacts on your thinking and bodily sensations

- you only start to be able to accurately assess your feared outcome if you test out your fears

- it is making you miss opportunities to learn that *you can cope*

- every time you run away you reinforce the idea that anxious thoughts and feelings are unbearable and must be avoided

- it is only through sticking with a scary situation that you learn that anxious feelings in your body run out of fuel if you can just ride the wave of anxious feelings and let them die out (see Chapter 6 for more information about this)

- you learned to be scared of this thing and you can unlearn that fear too

- being so scared of something that it interferes with your life is really rubbish, but on the flip side overcoming a fear is one of the best feelings ever! Your confidence will soar.

Exposure – how does it work?

In days gone by, psychologists used something called "flooding" to help people manage their fears. As avoiding things teaches us that we cannot cope, that the anxiety is unbearable and the feared thing is going to "get us" in some way, psychologists thought, "Right, well, we will do the opposite: instead of avoiding we will drown in the feared thing." If someone was terrified of spiders, it was thought that sticking them in a room full of big, hairy, black spiders would mean that their anxiety would peak and then begin to die out as they realised that the spiders didn't actually crawl up their nose, bite them on the bum, or do them any harm at all. For some people, this worked well; but for lots of people it didn't. Nothing works for everyone, but this was quite a high-risk strategy because if the person ended up running screaming from the room, then their confidence was shattered and it gave weight to the anxious belief "I cannot cope". We imagine that psychologists who worked on this idea of flooding had much shorter waiting lists and lots of free time as flooding is a pretty hard sell for someone with a strong fear. If you are very motivated to get rid of a phobia then this might work for you, but these days we work with what we call "exposure" in a more gradual way as this is what the research tells us is most effective.

Graded exposure allows us to work with more manageable levels of fear and anxiety and means we get to learn about our bodily sensations, the rise and fall of our anxiety levels, and keep track of our anxious thoughts whilst we are working towards overcoming a fear.

The idea is that we have a clear goal (e.g. if you are scared of dogs, it might be being able to stroke a friend's large dog), and we work backwards from this goal to see what we can manage and how we can challenge ourselves to increase how close we get to the feared thing and use all our positive coping strategies (plus some treats and rewards) to allow us to face the fear bit by bit. You might start with stroking a cute little puppy and work up gradually through a range of breeds until you get to your friend's St Bernard. Of course, this means you need access to quite a lot of dogs! You might pay a visit to your local dogs' home and enlist their help.

Usually when someone develops a strong fear, it starts off with feeling scared of the possible outcomes of that actual event or situation (e.g. being laughed at if you put your hand up in class); but then we end up most scared of our anxious responses. The bodily sensations of being dizzy, sweating and feeling a bit "unreal" is so unnerving that we can't even think about contributing in class as we don't want to kick off this awful feeling. Another good example is being scared of injections. Quite often it is not the "sharp scratch" that a person scared of needles is desperate to avoid so much as the overwhelming anxiety that comes whilst lining up waiting for an injection at school or sitting in the doctor's waiting room. Some level of anxiety is completely normal as injections are not fun and pain free, but if you feel like you can't have important injections or you are losing many nights' sleep over them, then this is now looking more like a phobia. With this particular phobia, you might need some help from your doctor or school nurse to get access to things that can be used to gradually expose you to the feared thing, including, perhaps, a clean needle, and maybe watching someone else getting an injection. So, if you have a fear of needles, how might you go about using exposure to overcome this fear?

GRADED EXPOSURE FOR FEAR OF INJECTIONS

End goal: to be able to get an injection at school with all my friends.

Steps on my exposure ladder

1. Look at drawings of syringes on the internet (Mum to find for me):1 out of 10 fear.

2. Look at drawings of people getting injections (cartoons): 1.5 out of 10 fear.

3. Look at photographs of syringes on the internet: 2 out of 10 fear.

4. Look at photographs of people getting injections on the internet: 2.5 out of 10 fear.

5. Watch a YouTube video of someone getting an injection: 5 out of 10 fear.

6. Watch a close-up video of a syringe entering someone's arm: 6.5 out of 10 fear.

7. Hold a sterile syringe in its packet: 7 out of 10 fear.

8. Watch my mum/a friend get an injection: 8 out of 10 fear.

9. End goal – get an injection at school with all my friends: 9 out of 10 fear.

Designing your own exposure ladder

So, where do you start? You start with your end goal and this needs to be something meaningful and important, because facing your fears can be tough and you need to feel motivated to do it. Make sure that your goal is clear and there is no confusion about what you want to be able to do. "Be OK near my friend's dog" doesn't really cut it and "Not be scared of needles" is too vague. The goals we have discussed so far in this chapter such as "Stroke Max, my friend Dave's big dog" is more like it or "Get my vaccination with all my friends at school". Think clearly identifiable behaviours and then think of a special treat or reward for yourself too – facing your fears is tough and you need to keep your motivation up. If you can get a trusted adult on board this really helps with rewards, but make sure you reward yourself even if you are going solo. A nice meal out with family or a close friend or a trip to see a film or exhibition that you really fancy are great rewards, but you need to pick things that are going to be motivating for you.

Now you have a clear end goal, you need to work out the rungs on your ladder. We rate how scary each step is on a scale of 0 to 10 (0 being no fear at all and 10 the most terrified ever), to be sure that we are not trying to jump too quickly from things that are not really that scary and challenging, to things that are much tougher to face. It needs to build up gradually so that each time you are tolerating a little bit more fear and anxiety and learning that it doesn't last forever, and that you can cope with both the scary thing and the anxious feelings. You can have between 8 and 12 steps on your ladder and usually it has about ten.

You need to decide exactly how long you are going to stay in your feared situation or what your "fear level" will be before you can quit. This often means staying in the feared situation for quite some time, up to an hour. We would usually say that you need to be rating your fear as less than 2 out of 10 before you can call it quits. If you are feeling anxious enough for it to still make you feel nervous when you think about doing that step again, then you need to stick with it for a bit longer. For some steps, it will be that you repeat them lots of times so that you can see and feel your anxious responses come down below 2 out of 10 before moving on to the next step, as you are not always able to control how long things happen for.

Personal experience – Phoebe

When I was treated for my anxiety, I was taught the method of "exposure". My main issue at the time was obsessions and compulsions so I used exposure to face the perceived fear and threat of not completing my rituals. I was very keen to get rid of all my rituals and was at first very startled by how long the process was taking. I made a list of all of my rituals and scored each one based on how uncomfortable and anxious it made me. I started out on the ones that made me least anxious and worked my way up to the bigger, more scary ones. I found that starting with the least scary ones gave me the confidence and sense of achievement to tackle the scarier ones. Every time I tackled a thought, an obsession or a compulsion, I became more confident that I could overcome my anxiety and eventually I did.

Safety behaviours

Psychologists talk about "safety behaviours" and this means things that we use to make our fears bearable. We might be OK stroking dogs as long as Mum is very close by, or we might always have a drink in our hand at parties so that we can grip onto it tightly. These "crutches" are OK at getting us through an anxious situation, but they can also prevent us from truly overcoming our fears as they are aimed at reducing the feelings of anxiety, not at changing the way that we think and behave in situations that we find scary. If we think, "I only managed that because Mum was there" then we are not learning that we can cope all on our own. The drink might stop us shaking (although it could also make it more obvious to others when we are shaking), but it also makes us believe that others seeing we are anxious would be a disaster when actually it is totally manageable. We need to get rid of safety behaviours as we need to *feel the fear* as we climb up the exposure ladder as this is the only way we learn that our anxiety will slowly start to be less and less, that we can manage, and that the feared thing doesn't (usually) happen. You might need to have a good think about all the things that you currently do in that situation and then work out if any of them are going to get in the way of you feeling the fear and learning from the process. Taking deep breaths can help to make your anxiety more manageable and having someone you trust with you is the same. These are acceptable behaviours to help you climb the ladder, but it might be that you include steps with someone you trust there and then increase your exposure to the fear by having steps where you do it alone.

Managing set-backs

Sometimes when we talk to young people about exposure they say, "I tried that and it hasn't worked." More often than not, there is a really good reason that it hasn't worked and it isn't because they are immune to the power of facing their fears. Exposure is not based on the idea that bad things never happen (sometimes they do) but what we learn through facing our fears is that the outcome we are scared of is not as likely to happen as we think it is, and that even when things go wrong we can cope well enough to pick ourselves up and carry on. Rather than breaking us, this can then make us feel more confident at handling fears and uncertain situations in the future.

There are some common set-backs that get in the way of successfully overcoming your fears through an exposure ladder. These include:

1. You don't really want to face the fear right now.

It is not a good idea to start trying to tackle a fear when you have a lot on. You need to have some time and not too many other pressures like exams or big changes in your life. If you are struggling to get going, maybe it's not the right time to start tackling your worries and you should not give yourself a hard time; just make a date (maybe after exams or during a holiday time) when you can re-assess your situation. Sometimes fears and phobias have their place in our lives, so even though it is a horrible feeling we might also get some reward for it. For example, if you are really scared of the dark, but this means that a parent or carer sits with you at bedtime, then you might not want to overcome this fear as overcoming it would mean that you miss out on some quality alone time with someone that you love who is usually very busy. The rewards for your phobia might not be so obvious, but there might be some there. Have a good think about what your fear means for you, because if there is a reason to hold on to a phobia, it might be that you can find other ways to get the reward without staying scared of stuff, or it might be that it is just not a priority to tackle it right now.

2. The goals are not realistic.

If you just have one thing that you are super scared of, then you probably just have to dive right in, but most people have a few. If you have started with something you are really terrified of then maybe it would be good to start with a smaller fear. If your rungs on your ladder are well spaced then this shouldn't be too much of a problem, but if your anxious thoughts are screaming at you, "It can't be done!" when you think about your goal, then maybe you need a smaller, more achievable goal for your first go at exposure.

3. The first rung on the ladder is too scary.

If you have something too scary on your first rung, it's hard to convince yourself to get started. You need to start with something that is barely scary at all then work your way up, with little rewards at every step. If you are getting stuck, try to break steps down further.

4. The rungs between the ladder are too far apart.

If you have big jumps between your steps, then you are likely to get stuck. If you are feeling 2 out of 10 scared of watching someone have an injection on YouTube and 8 out of 10 watching your friend get an injection, then there need to be lots of steps in between to build your confidence and help you learn that anxiety will go down and that you can cope with it. It can be that you are not used to rating anxiety on a 0 to 10 scale so are not rating your fear very accurately. It's fine to keep revising your ladder and adding steps or moving things around.

5. You are trying to move up the ladder too quickly.

This is when you are eager to get ahead but forget that exposure is all about gradually allowing your anxiety to come down and learning that you can cope. If you manage a step then you can't just think, "Phew, I am so glad that is over" and move on to the next one; you need to feel like it is now a piece of cake and you could do it again in a flash. If you don't feel like this, then you haven't done that step for long enough or enough times.

6. Powerful anxious thoughts are getting in the way.

You might need to read the next chapter before you can crack on with your exposure. If your head is running wild with "I can't cope", "I'm useless", "I'm going to die" then you are unlikely to be able to stick with the situation and feel the anxiety come down. You need to be able to identify the anxious thoughts and have some positive coping statements or more helpful alternatives handy, so that you can calm your anxious mind and feel more in control.

4

Tackling Anxious Thoughts

So, we know that when we are feeling under threat, it changes the way that we think. This is because through evolution our brain has developed so that our complex thinking is shut down when we are experiencing a threat. Complex thinking is too slow for dealing with threats. A caveman would not be well served by spending his time thinking about how the other caveman is feeling and what his "motivation" might be if that caveman is coming at him with a big club. Our brains are designed so that when we are under threat we make decisions about our responses quickly and based on the least possible information. Flight, fight and freeze are our three options. Three options are a reasonable number for our anxious brain to deal with.

Another important thing happens when we feel under threat. We have evolved to focus all our attention on the possible threats and where they might be coming from. It is a bit daft noticing the beautiful sunset if there is a sabre tooth tiger hiding in the bushes. This means that when we are anxious, we can miss important information in our surroundings as we are so focused on the things we find worrying or scary.

Outsmarting evolution

The problem that we have is that your friend's birthday party is a very different situation from the one the caveman was facing. I really hope no one at the party is coming at you in a loin cloth with a club or has brought their pet sabre tooth with them. If they are, you are going to the wrong parties! The kinds of threats we deal with these days are much more complicated and often involve social situations.

THE REGISTER BY ANTHONY

Scraping chairs echoing through the walls tell the world that lessons are starting. People sit down, get their work out, all standard. But then the teacher begins to speak in that monotonous, repetitive tone and the only other thing I can hear is my own breathing.

Adams.

At least it's alphabetical. I've got at least a minute before it's my turn. A minute of my head spinning, my heart pounding as I try and figure out what I should say and how I should say it. "Yes, sir?" Or would "Here" be better? What is everyone else saying?

Dawson.

It's getting harder to think properly – is everyone staring at me? Looking up to find out is out of the question right now.

Hardy.

I need to take a moment. Remove myself from the situation, close my eyes and imagine myself leaving my body behind and just getting up, going outside for some fresh air and focusing on my breathing. Counting my breaths in, holding it, breathing out. I find I can open my eyes again. The sound of my breathing is fading into its normal, quieter space of my mind. And when my name comes, I have a voice again.

'Yes, sir.'

It isn't much use telling you, or you telling yourself, "Don't be anxious, it will only make things worse." If that worked, we wouldn't have bothered writing this book. What we need to be able to do is break the anxious cycle, like the one we described at the party in the previous chapter. We can do this in several ways, and one of them is to be able to notice and *evaluate* our thoughts. Then, if they are based on faulty information or just plain unhelpful, we can try to replace them with more helpful, realistic and positive alternatives.

Our brain has evolved lots of brilliant helpful shortcuts so we can think smart, not hard, and make sense of the incredible and complex social world that we live in. The problem is that these shortcuts can be hijacked very effectively by our anxiety to make us "anxious thinkers" rather than "smart thinkers".

It is important that we are aware of the kind of thinking that can trip us up when we are feeling anxious, otherwise these anxious thoughts and shortcuts can make us feel awful and provoke more anxious responses in our bodies, which make us more likely to respond with angry or avoidant behaviours.

We can tackle these thoughts head on and then make different choices about how to respond. It is important to remember that when we feel bad, we think "bad" (the fancy name for this is "emotional reasoning") and although these thoughts are not facts, we can often treat them as though they are *true*, because they just feel right. Because lots of the shortcuts are helpful to our thinking when we are doing OK, then we are not even aware of them. The ten "errors" outlined below are to help you spot when anxiety is tricking you, or the shortcuts are being hijacked by your anxiety and becoming unhelpful:

- *Catastrophising* – this is when we think about something that worries us and we keep going with "what if" until we reach a total catastrophe: for example, you do badly on a test and from this decide that you will lose the respect of your teacher, fail the whole year and never get a good job. This can feel like getting stuck on a track that it is very hard to turn away from even though you know it won't take you anywhere good. This "error" is more about how we think than what we think and could be a good description of worrying or rumination. We will look at ways to work with worry in detail in the next chapter.

- *Jumping to conclusions* – our threat brain does not have resources to analyse all the information when we are under threat (think about the caveman wondering about the daily calorie intake of the sabre tooth tiger) so rather than waiting to see all the information, we use a small amount of information to make a judgement and we come down on the side of caution. This is our safest option. However, if a friend approaches us looking fed up and a bit cross and we use this information alone rather than waiting to hear what they are going to say, we jump to the conclusion they are cross with us and that it is going to be an unpleasant interaction (making it highly likely we will quickly make our excuses and avoid them).

- *Taking things personally* – when we are doing well, humans usually blame the universe for the bad things that happen and take personal credit for when good things happen. It helps us to stay healthy and happy. However, anxious thinking means that we can start to blame ourselves for things that have very little or nothing to do with us. For example, your mum or dad is in a bad mood and rather than thinking about all the other things that could be to blame (stress at work, feeling unwell, worrying about money), you decide that they are fed up with you and that you make them miserable.

- *Negative filtering/gloomy glasses* – this happens when we ignore all the good stuff that has happened and focus on the bad things. You might be preoccupied with something you said in class that you felt was stupid and think, "I made a fool of myself today" whilst ignoring the fact that no one laughed at you or even responded to what you said and that everyone was friendly to you at lunch. The negative filter can mean we make a judgement about the whole day and ourselves based on only a small amount of negative information and this focus makes us feel horrible. Our brains are tuning in to the negative to keep us safe, but it really ruins your day.

- *Over-generalising* – a lot like the negative filter, this means we use one event or piece of information about something specific to make a global judgement. For example, I didn't get invited to a party on Saturday so everybody hates me.

- *Over-estimating* – we over-estimate the likelihood that bad things will happen. We could call this "better to be safe than sorry" reasoning. It makes us more cautious, which if the world is dangerous is really helpful; but when it's just our anxious brain tricking us, it can make life difficult.

- *Mind reading* – being a human is all about relating to other humans. We are designed and programmed to want to be known and to know other people. However, this important and pretty wonderful bit of being a human can mean we (wrongly) think that we can read people's minds and, because we are thinking negatively, we assume they are too. We can then misinterpret intentions and behaviour in a way that is really unhelpful. For example, if a person is looking at you on a bus you might think, "They are judging me, they think I look weird" when you have absolutely no idea what they are actually thinking. They could be admiring your shoes or coat or they could simply be staring straight through you worrying about what other people on the bus are thinking of them. This kind of anxious mind reading makes us feel awful and has no basis in reality.

- *Fortune telling* – just like relating to other people, working out what might happen next is also what makes us the dominant species on Earth. It allows us to solve problems and be creative and inventive. The problem can be that when we are feeling anxious and believe we already know what the future holds, we can begin thinking that we don't need to try things out. Why would you go and talk to that interesting-looking person if you already know that they are going to hate you?

- *Labelling* – we need to have quick ways to make sense of the world around us so that we can make decisions efficiently and effectively. If we can assess a situation and quickly give it a label, then this can help us quickly make sense of what is going on and then choose the best option: "I am safe" or "This is not OK". When we are having a difficult experience, we label it or ourselves. For example, you forget to call a friend on their birthday and you think, "I am a useless friend" or even "I am useless".

- *Black-and-white thinking* – just like labelling, cate-gorising things as either "brilliant" or "terrible" is a good way to make quick decisions and reason efficiently when there is lots of information. It takes time to think about the complexities of people and situations and we don't always have lots of time, especially when we are anxious. If we rely on this kind of thinking, then we can get into trouble. An example of this might be, "She is good at talking to people and I'm no good at talking to people" rather than recognising that there are grey areas; talking to other people is a complex skill. A more complex or grey way of thinking about this could be, "I am good at talking to people one to one or when there are not too many people around, but find it harder in a large group".

Catching thoughts

So, now we have some ideas for identifying whether anxiety has hijacked our shortcuts for making sense of the world; and we may recognise any of the errors above in our thinking. We now also need to be able to "catch" our thoughts when we are feeling anxious and have a good look at them in the cold light of day. Once we have got a hold (and a record) of our thoughts when we are anxious, we can start to examine them to see if we are using too many anxious shortcuts and spot any themes to our anxious thinking. We can also start to think about whether there are more balanced and helpful ways of thinking that we might be able to use in these situations.

It can be useful to keep a notebook or "thought diary" with you, and start to notice and write down both what is going on and your exact thoughts at times when you are stressed or feeling anxious. You can then use some simple questions to help you work out what shortcuts your anxious mind might be using and, rather than simply accepting them as true, we can challenge these thoughts to see if they stand up to scrutiny.

Catching thoughts can feel odd at first. It requires us to pay close attention to processes that are usually automatic and be mindful of our own minds and thinking. The ideas in Chapter 6 will help you think about being mindful in lots of ways. To help you get into the habit of thinking about your thoughts more, you might want to set a reminder on your phone every 30 minutes for a day and think about what has been going through your mind and remembering any anxious thoughts. Alternatively, it might be that you ask someone you trust to remind you whenever you are anxious to write down exactly what is going on and what you are thinking at the time. If you wait too long, then it can be very hard to remember what was going through your head when you were feeling anxious. Often people say things like, "I don't think anything, my head is just a mess" or, "My thoughts go too fast when I am anxious. I can't remember what I think." It takes some time to be aware and mindful of what is going on with our thoughts when we feel anxious.

Personal experience – Phoebe

I always described this sensation as having a "washing-machine brain" because I felt as though my head was a flurry of thoughts and feelings that I couldn't grasp or single out. I used this phrase to explain the sensation to others and, over time, developed my ability to capture thoughts out of the washing machine so I could take them out and analyse them.

Sometimes when people try to catch thoughts, they write down feelings rather than thoughts: "I feel rubbish" or "This is horrible". This can reflect how hard it is to recognise the important thoughts in an anxious situation. You do feel rubbish when you are anxious, it is not a positive feeling, but this isn't usually the most important thought and is more about the anxious feelings. The most important anxious thoughts to be able to recognise and challenge are usually a global statement about you as a person: what we sometimes call a "hot thought" because it has a very immediate emotional response. We believe it intensely, with our anxious feelings making it feel right or true. These thoughts can be so intense that we try to avoid or ignore them.

Personal experience – Phoebe

For a long time, I shut away unhelpful and self-critical thoughts. It's poisonous. It doesn't solve the problem. I learnt the hard way that the only way to overcome these thoughts is to face them.

Challenging thoughts

Once you have caught your anxious thoughts, it would be a good idea to take time to sit down and make sense of your ways of thinking and challenge them.

Imagine you are at work or school getting some lunch. You are alone, it is busy and you start to feel self-conscious. You can feel your cheeks getting hotter and your hands starting to get sweaty. Your heart is pounding in your chest and you think, "Everyone is staring at me. I look an anxious mess." This immediately sends your anxious feelings through the roof and your cheeks flush hotter and your hands start to shake. You don't want to pick up the tray in case people can see your hands shaking. You decide to get out of there quickly and make a run for the toilets. In the toilet, you think, "I am pathetic" and you feel too anxious to go back into the cafeteria.

What can we do with that thought?

First, we need to take a few deep breaths to try to calm our threat system so we are able to think straight.

Then we need a chance to look carefully at the thought and ask ourselves, "How much do I believe this?" We really need to answer this question in the moment, so you will need this as a column in your thought record or a prompt in your diary.

What is the situation?	What is the thought?	How much do I believe this?	What is the evidence? Can I spot an error?	How much do I believe it now? (%)	What would be a more accurate or helpful thought?	How anxious do you feel on a scale of 0 to 10?
In the cafeteria getting my lunch.	Everyone is staring at me. I look an anxious mess.	99%	Supporting evidence: one person gave me a funny look. I feel terrible. Evidence against: The new boy asked me a question. I was staring at my feet a lot so can't be sure who was looking. Errors: jumping to conclusions, mind reading, taking things personall, negative filter.	30%	I am feeling anxious but I am doing OK. That person could be thinking about anything.	3

Table 4.1 Example thought record/diary

What's the evidence?

Sometimes we talk about "being a detective" and seeking out all the evidence we can find for and against the thought. We might need some help with this and if you can work with someone you trust this is usually very helpful. If you are challenging your thoughts alone, then try to imagine what a person you trust might say, or turn it on its head and think what you might say to someone you care about who was thinking this way in this situation. Most of us are much kinder to our friends than we are to ourselves. You might say to a friend, "You can't know what other people are thinking and they don't know what you are thinking or feeling! It never looks as bad as you think it does" or, "Who cares what they think, you are doing great." In Chapter 7, we also use imagery (see the Soothing Other exercise) that can help you to imagine what someone being wise and understanding might say to you.

Anxious thought	Anxious shortcut	Alternative/helpful thought
I can't cope	Fortune telling	Just because I am feeling anxious does not mean I can't do OK.
I am going to die	Over-generalising Over-estimating	I feel really awful right now but I have felt this way before and anxiety will not do me harm. I need to wait for it to pass.
I am stupid	Labelling Over-generalising Black-and-white thinking	I made a mistake and that's OK.
I am going to mess this up	Fortune telling Catastrophising	I am going to be brave and give this a go even though my anxiety is giving me a really hard time.
Everyone is staring at me; I look a mess	Jumping to conclusions Over-generalising	I might look a bit anxious but everyone gets anxious.

Table 4.2 Some ideas of alternative or helpful thoughts

So, this is complicated. Let's recap.

The process is to catch the thought, write it down exactly as it comes into your head and make a note of what the situation was. Rate how much you believe it and make a note of how anxious you feel on a scale of 0 to 10. Then look at the thought and try to see if there is any evidence that supports it and any evidence that might indicate it's not true or not an accurate reflection of the situation. Look out for any of the anxious shortcuts that we outlined above and make a note of that. Noting down the kind of anxious shortcuts not only helps you to find more balanced thoughts but also means you can start to spot themes in your thinking that can help you to challenge thoughts in the moment rather than writing everything down. Our shortcuts can also point us to how it might look if we were being more objective, for example, if I am jumping to conclusions, where can I seek more evidence? If I am being black and white, where is the grey area? Always come back to, "What would my mum or best friend say about this situation?" as taking a new perspective can be most helpful in coming up with your more balanced thought.

Once you have gone through this process, then rate how much you now believe the thought (as a percentage) and also rate how anxious you feel out of ten. The final step is to make a note of how anxious you feel. This allows you to see if the process of thought challenging is having any impact on your level of anxiety.

Catching and challenging thoughts in your notebook/diary

1. Write down the exact thought in quotation marks and give a short explanation of the context.

I thought, "Everyone hates me" as I was walking to the toilet at the party.

2. Rate how much you believe it.

   I really believe this thought 90 per cent.

3. Rate how anxious you feel.

   I feel/felt very anxious, about 8 out of 10; I was sweating and felt dizzy and sick.

4. Then think about the evidence.

   For: Katie Jones didn't say hello. No one has come over to talk to me yet.

   Against: Jack Smith smiled at me when I came in. Jessica invited me to the party.

   What would my mum say? She would say I need to stick it out and see what happens; she would say I am feeling anxious and need to take a deep breath and find a friendly face.

5. Spot any possible anxious shortcuts.

   I am jumping to conclusions as I have not been at the party very long; I am taking things personally as Katie ignoring me could be nothing to do with me; I am catastrophising and over-generalising from one negative interaction.

6. Rate how much you believe the thought now.

   I believe this thought 40 per cent.

7. Rate how anxious you feel.

I don't feel too bad now, about 4 out of 10.

8. What would a more balanced thought be?

People are not always welcoming and friendly for lots of reasons, but I can cope with this if I take a deep breath and look out for a friendly face.

There are benefits of using a thought record sheet as it is brief, easily transportable, and gives you all the right prompts. However, a notebook means you can write in it any time and no one needs to know what you are doing. You can also write as much as you like, as you are not limited on space. You can use whatever suits you; you might use both.

The idea is that you can do this with someone you trust, but if no one is around then you can do it by yourself too. As you get more practice at looking for evidence and seeing the biases in your thinking, it becomes automatic and you will no longer need the sheet or diary. You will be less likely to just trust your anxious thoughts and will begin to recognise that a lot of the time you are thinking negatively because you feel anxious, not because things truly are bad.

Having said that, it isn't always the case that challenging a thought makes you feel less anxious. Sometimes it might set you off catastrophising, especially if you are alone and still feeling very anxious. It can be hard at first. Please don't let this put you off. Find someone who can help, and keep on having a go. Changing the way you think is not an easy thing to do and it will take time and practice. If you think this sounds helpful and commit to this way of approaching your thoughts, we really believe it can break the anxious cycle and help you to outsmart evolution, so you are feeling more in control when your anxious thoughts try to take you down an unhelpful track.

Personal experience - Phoebe

When I started to write down replacement thoughts for my anxious thoughts, I thought I would never believe them; but over time, the balanced replacement thoughts seemed more and more rational and now they are the ones my brain gravitates towards most often.

Positive coping thoughts and cheerleading

When we feel bad, we think bad. We can start to talk to ourselves in a negative way, criticising ourselves and pointing out mistakes or flaws. This can be a very damaging habit to develop. We do this more, and are more critical, when we have had other people saying horrible things to us. Sadly, this can be a parent or a teacher, brother or sister, or maybe someone has been bullying you at school. These negative voices can end up being the voice that we talk to ourselves with a lot of the time. Then, when we make a mistake, instead of recognising that we all make mistakes and that they are part of life, we might say, "Well, of course I messed up, I am a mess!" or even worse, when we start to feel anxious they say, "Look at you, you're pathetic, you can't cope with anything!" which plays right into the anxious cycle.

We all do this to some extent and it is a big part of many cultures to be modest and minimise our achievements. If this becomes our main way of talking to ourselves, however, these critical voices can really play into the anxiety cycle and make us feel anxious and sometimes even hopeless.

To counteract this "negative self-talk", we don't always need to catch our thoughts and challenge them. Lots of young people find it really helpful to find coping thoughts and cheerleading statements to carry with them or stick all over their walls. To find your own coping statements and cheerleading statements, you might look at quotes from the internet, song lyrics, or you might look to religious texts for inspiration. It becomes easier and more natural as you practise and they are there ready to jump to the front of your mind and divert you from the negative self-talk.

COPING STATEMENTS

☆ "Just because I am anxious does not mean I cannot manage this situation just fine."

☆ "This feeling will pass."

☆ "It is natural to feel like this. I didn't choose, or want this feeling, but I'm stuck with it for a while until it passes. I can just cope the best that I can."

☆ "I have got through this before, I will get through it again."

☆ "It's OK not to be OK."

☆ "Everyone makes mistakes: they are like teachers, it's how we learn."

☆ "Anxiety makes me feel horrible, but it won't do me any harm."

☆ "I am not my thoughts."

☆ "I don't have to give these anxious thoughts love and attention. I am going to be kind to myself instead."

Using coping statements can be a quick and effective way of improving anxiety, especially if you are working hard on facing your fears using exposure. In the next chapter, we will think more about how to work with worry, and the ways we can try to interrupt an anxious track of thinking.

❧ 5 ❧

Tackling Worries

When should I worry about worry?

Worrying is sometimes useful. Worrying is a thought process: "What if...", but because it focuses on negative outcomes it has a strong emotional aspect too. Despite it feeling bad, lots of people value worry. They think if they don't worry then bad things will happen (and as we have already said, to some extent this can be true). We know that problems arise when we hold both strongly positive ideas about worry, for example, "Worrying means I will avoid bad things" alongside negative ideas about worry, for example, "Worrying too much will make me go mad." What can then happen is that we worry more because we think that it is helpful, but also worry about that worry and feel negatively about it. Complicated.

Worry becomes a problem when you are spending lots of time worrying and it starts to interfere with doing other things; and when we start to get lots of physical symptoms with the worry, such as headaches, stomach aches, muscle pain.

What can I do to make my worry less worrying?

SERENITY PRAYER

Grant me the SERENITY to
accept the things I cannot change,
The COURAGE to change the
things I can;
and the WISDOM to
know the difference.

Distraction

We only have a limited amount of space in our heads for processing our thoughts; it is very hard to think about two things at once! So, one of the best ways to deal with worries is to take up that space with other thoughts.

Focused distraction

To stop worrying, we can use a difficult task that takes up a lot of mental energy and doesn't allow us to think about our worry. We just do this for a short amount of time to interrupt the "what if" train we get carried away on when we worry. A good example of this is counting backwards from 1000 in threes for two minutes. Set an alarm on your phone and furrow your brow. If you are a maths genius, you might need to find a more complicated operation to keep your brain fully occupied.

Personal experience - Phoebe

Sometimes I will look around the room and notice how many things there are, for example, there are three pencils, two windows and one door. Finding three of something, then two of something and then one can be very helpful to ground myself and take my mind off racing thoughts.

Distracting activities

Another way of interrupting the cycle is to throw yourself into an activity that will require some concentration and that starts to work on the bad feelings that often go along with worry (such as tense feelings in your body). It is useful to have a range of distracting activities that you enjoy and make you feel good that you can try when you are struggling with worries. This might be creative (drawing or crochet) or it might be physical (kicking a ball at the wall or going for a jog). It is often true that worries get bigger and more troublesome at night when there is not much to do and less that can take your mind off them, so make sure some of the things on your list are things you can do alone and without making too much noise! Complicated adult colouring books or Sudoku puzzles can be helpful or you might try listening to an audio book or music on your headphones.

Personal experience - Phoebe

Over the years I have utilised many distracting activities. For me these include knitting, sewing, cycling and découpage. These activities are different for everyone, so find what works for you personally.

Personal experience – David

I started to run and this was a major factor in reducing my anxiety. Running just provided an instant release from feeling anxious and created a calm over my mind, reduced my tendency to overthink and also made me feel tired and relaxed at night, which helped me drift off to sleep.

EXAMPLE LIST OF DISTRACTIONS FROM A 14-YEAR-OLD GIRL

☆ practising the piano

☆ playing a board game with my older brother

☆ cooking with my parents

☆ writing a song or poem

☆ going for a walk with the dog (and asking Dad)

☆ phoning a close friend for a chat

☆ learning to do a new hairstyle "up-do" from the internet.

You will notice that a lot of these ideas involve another important person as usually this is helpful in keeping our attention off our anxieties. We also know that one of the best ways to feel better when we are struggling is being close to someone we care about and feel safe with.

Protected worry time

If we are accepting that worry is normal, and even useful sometimes, but is taking up too much time or popping up at unhelpful times, one solution is to make a protected worry time. This might be ten minutes every day or 30 minutes once a week. It really is whatever feels best for you. Of course, worries will pop into your head outside of this time, but the idea is that you notice and acknowledge them as worries, "I am having a worry or a worrying thought" (mindfulness strategies outlined in Chapter 6 might help with this). You might even write a quick note to yourself if it feels like an important worry, but then tell yourself, "I will think about this during worry time tonight at 7pm" or whenever your chosen worry time will be. This can be helpful in allowing you to let worries go if they come along at a time when you need to focus on something else, or the anxious feelings that often come along with the worry might be problematic. Worry time should be in a place and at a time when you feel calm and safe. Ideally, worry time should be a chance to talk to someone you trust and feel safe with, so you can share worries and talk things through. Some people are not lucky enough to have a trusted adult or friend who can help them with this, but it can still be helpful to try out the idea of protected worry time where you write worries down and work through them logically and systematically.

Worry box

A worry box is somewhere that you can put your worries if you don't want to forget them (although usually forgetting them isn't a bad thing!). It can help you to feel more contained when you have a big worry but want to wait until protected worry time or until you get a chance to sort and share your worries (see the next paragraph). You might want to decorate a shoe box (this could be a good distracting activity if you are worrying) or you might be able to buy a box with a lock on it. If you use a shoe box, then just cut a hole in the top so it is big enough to post paper through, but not so that you can easily get them out. You can also give the worry box to a trusted person to take care of so that they are in charge of your worries for a bit and you can get on with a distracting activity.

Sharing and sorting worries

You might have heard the old saying, "A problem shared is a problem halved." We really think this is the case. When we sort and share worries, just like protected worry time, this usually involves a trusted other person. However, you can still sort your worries even if there is not someone you want to share worries with. Sorting worries means writing all your worries down and sorting them into groups. It can be helpful to put each worry on a post-it note, so you can group them together, or you might just have two columns on the page.

Worries that I can tackle	Worries that I can do nothing about
I am worried about how I will get to my music exam.	Worrying about what other people think of me at school.
Worrying I upset my best friend when I left the party early.	Worrying about my brother/mum/partner getting poorly or having an accident.
Fear of dogs.	Worrying about whether my university application will be accepted.
I won't get my coursework in on time.	Seeing a photo of someone I had a relationship with on a date with someone else and worrying they are more attractive and fun than me.

Table 5.1 Worries that I can tackle and worries that I can do nothing about

Sorting is the start of accepting the things we cannot change and changing the things that we can accept, as in the Serenity Prayer. Sorting helps you to feel more in control and if you do it with someone else then it means you are sharing your problems, which is sometimes enough to make them seem smaller or even so unimportant that they disappear.

Problem solving

So, some of our worries might be things that we need to do something about. For example, if you are worrying a lot about how to get to your music exam then you could do some problem solving. "I don't know what bus to get or whether I can get off near the venue or I might have to walk a bit. How will I know where to go?" This is when it can be helpful to "problem solve".

Steps to problem solving

Step 1: Write down all possible solutions, no matter how daft:

☆ Don't bother going/cancel.

☆ Ask my dad to drive me.

☆ Use a journey-planning app to find out the route.

☆ Ask a friend to come with me so they can help if I get lost.

☆ Just set off to the bus stop and hope for the best.

☆ Ask someone to do a practice run with me to the venue the weekend before my exam.

Step 2: Write down the pros and cons of each possible solution:

PROS OF NOT BOTHERING AND CANCELLING:

☆ Reduce my stress.

☆ Don't have to do any more practice.

☆ Won't have to ask anyone for help.

CONS OF NOT BOTHERING AND CANCELLING:

☆ I would feel disappointed.

☆ All my practice to now has gone to waste.

☆ I will miss out on an opportunity.

☆ My music teacher will be very disappointed.

☆ I won't be able to move on to the next grade.

Conclusion: too extreme. Not a helpful solution.

PROS OF ASKING DAD TO DRIVE ME:

☆ Don't have to worry about public transport or walking very far.

☆ Dad could help me to manage my anxiety about the exam in the car.

☆ Free.

CONS OF ASKING DAD TO DRIVE ME:

☆ Dad is really busy and might be late to collect me and I would get stressed.

☆ I would feel like a child and I want to be more independent.

Conclusion: not a bad solution. A possible answer.

PROS OF USING A JOURNEY-PLANNING APP:

☆ I would be independent.

☆ I would learn a new skill.

☆ It will tell me exactly how long
the journey will take.

CONS OF USING A JOURNEY-PLANNING APP:

☆ I don't trust an app; it could go wrong
so this might increase my anxiety.

☆ If my phone dies I would not know where to walk.

☆ No one will be with me if I need some help.

Conclusion: a possibility.

**PROS OF ASKING A FRIEND TO COME
WITH ME IN CASE I GET LOST:**

☆ If I ask Jenny she is great at directions
and will ask someone if we need
to. I will feel more confident.

☆ I will have someone to chat to and distract me.

**CONS OF ASKING A FRIEND TO COME
WITH ME IN CASE I GET LOST:**

☆ I am not being independent.

☆ I would be missing an opportunity
to learn something new.

*Conclusion: not a bad solution but
doesn't seem the best one.*

PROS OF JUST SETTING OFF FOR THE BUS STOP AND HOPING FOR THE BEST:

☆ I might learn that actually people are helpful when
you are lost and I can cope with uncertainty.

☆ Don't need to do any planning or preparation.

CONS OF JUST SETTING OFF FOR THE BUS STOP AND HOPING FOR THE BEST:

☆ A music exam is important and not the
best time for trying something risky.

☆ I would probably feel very stressed.

☆ I might never get to the exam.

*Conclusion: not a good solution.
Too much stress and too much risk.*

PROS OF A PRACTICE RUN WITH A FRIEND THE WEEKEND BEFORE:

☆ I will feel secure on the day of the exam.

☆ We can make it into a fun trip out if I
find other things to do in that area.

☆ I can spend time with a friend
whom I have fun with.

☆ I will be independent on the day of
the exam, which feels important.

☆ I can use the travel app and learn a new skill.

**CONS OF A PRACTICE RUN WITH A
FRIEND THE WEEKEND BEFORE:**

☆ It takes quite a lot of time when I could
be practising for my exam.

☆ I am worried that the friend will think I am
overly anxious practising the route.

*Conclusion: this is the best solution
and I feel happy with it.*

Systematically working through problems like this takes a lot less time than you think, and if you are short on time just pick your top three solutions as often there are some that are clearly not going to work (for example, "just not bothering" was probably never going to be a solution). We find it helpful as important themes can jump out at you. In this example, the idea about independence seems to be key. Finding a balance between being prepared and supported and feeling like you are able to take care of yourself is often important to consider. Just knowing that there are a few solutions that are workable can make you feel less anxious as you have a back-up plan. Worrying "What if the app breaks?

What if Dad is late?" can make you feel awful; finding the best solution for you, involving those who need to be involved, and then making a clear plan, is the best way to manage these kinds of worries.

If you are still worrying and feeling anxious then the next step can be to make a plan of exactly how you will carry out the solution. For example:

I need to:

- pick a day

- choose a friend and ask them to come with me

- get the address and postcode

- download the map app

- plan the route

- plan a nice activity to do with the friend on that day in that area.

There might be some things you want to talk through or practise, for example, exactly how you will ask the friend and explain how and why you would like their help.

Flush them all away

Life is full of uncertainties. We don't know what is going to happen next and this makes life exciting, but can also make us feel anxious. Some of our worries might feel very important and hard to let go of even though we have put them in the "accept the things we cannot change" pile. One of the ways young people can give themselves permission to "let go" is to write the worries on toilet roll and then flush them down the toilet.

Personal experience - Phoebe

In the past, I have written all my worries onto a balloon and let it fly away outside. This was my way of letting go of my anxieties.

Worry is normal and everyone has worries. Sometimes we get really good at "catastrophising" and the "what ifs" quickly take us to the worst possible outcome. Sometimes we get stuck thinking a lot about bad things that could happen and this can take over and mean we can't think straight and even start to feel physically unwell. We hope that the ideas in this chapter can help you to accept the things that we cannot change and changing the things that we can accept, so you feel more able to let some worries go and come to helpful solutions when they are possible. We think the ideas in the next chapter will really help with letting worries go, so if you are struggling with acceptance then we suggest you keep reading.

One last thought ...

The ideas from CBT about how to tackle anxiety are a bit different from the ideas we talk about in Chapters 6 and 7. CBT focuses on challenging our anxieties head on, when sometimes people find that using techniques such as mindfulness (Chapter 6) and self-soothing (Chapter 7) strategies are more useful for them than these direct strategies.

Everyone is different and we wanted you to have ideas about lots of different ways that you can manage anxious thoughts, feelings and behaviours, so that you can choose the way that suits you best. Sometimes we might be feeling very agitated and threatened, and trying the "head on" techniques could feel too much. At times like these, you need to take a more compassionate approach to yourself and your thoughts. At other times, when you are feeling calmer and more able to focus, it can be helpful to sit down with a trusted adult (or alone with your handbook) and spend some time challenging thoughts and making plans about how to respond to anxieties. Quite often when we are feeling under threat and in our "flight/fight/freeze" state we cannot get full access to our thinking brain, so we need to soothe our threat system (Chapter 7) before we can get our thinking brain back online and start to think about using the approaches outlined in this chapter and those in Chapters 4 and 5.

The way that you choose to manage your anxiety will be different when managing different situations or may change at different times in your life, depending on the kinds of stresses that you are dealing with. Sometimes it may seem that one approach just fits better with you and the way you do things.

❧ 6 ❧

Being Mindful

Do you ever feel like your *mind* is *full* of worries about what's happened in the past or could in the future? Sometimes we have so many things in our minds that it can seem like never-ending noise, a whirlwind or even a washing machine!

Mindfulness is a technique that can help us to calm our thoughts and focus on the present moment. This means that we try to think about the here and now, and not the past or future. If thoughts are racing around your mind, you may feel anxious, worried, overwhelmed or stressed. It can be useful to take some time to just "be aware" in the present moment, accepting what is happening around you. Mindfulness is quite different from relaxation, although it can lead to you feeling more relaxed. With mindfulness, the goal is to focus your mind and be more aware of what you are experiencing; whereas with relaxation, the goal is simply to relax or release a tense body or mind.

To observe the present moment fully, you should try to be aware of your five senses. Try to think of what you are noticing as if it's a brand-new experience. So you might ask yourself, "What can I hear? Smell? Taste? See? Feel?" During this act of mindfulness, any thoughts that pass in your head should be acknowledged and accepted, but not thought about or acted on (allow them to drift in and out of your mind). Bring yourself back to the present moment gently, try not to be hard on yourself. Don't judge your thoughts as "good" or "bad" – they just "are". Mindfulness is a different way of dealing with anxious thoughts and feelings from CBT, as when we are being mindful we accept and let go of thoughts, rather than catching and evaluating them. If we keep our attention on, and accept what is happening in the moment, it can lead us to feel calmer, and more in control. We can then learn to respond in a more helpful way to what is happening around us.

As well as anxiety, mindfulness can help with:

- low mood / feeling sad

- anger

- relationship problems

- stress

- physical difficulties and pain (even cold and flu!).

Perhaps one of the most important things about mindfulness is that it takes practice. You might not get it quite right the first time, or the second, but if you keep practising you will, we hope, find that you can do it more easily and that it starts to help. Don't feel that you have failed if you don't do it perfectly the first few times – no one does!

Personal experience – Josh

Mindfulness and the breathing techniques associated with it were something I was always a bit sceptical about, but can now count them as a daily practice and something that has proved invaluable. It has helped me take control of my over-active, over-thinking mind.

Mindfulness is about focusing on the present moment, focusing our minds on something very separate from our worries and difficulties. To help us to do this, we choose to focus on one of our senses at a time.

Here is a helpful exercise for you to try:

Mindfulness exercise 1: Mindfulness of eating (chocolate buttons)

(You can also do this exercise with raisins or any small pieces of food.)

1. Hold the chocolate button between your thumb and fingers.

2. Bring your attention to the chocolate button, looking at it carefully as if you have never, ever seen one before.

   What can you see? What colours can you see? Is it dark or light? Look at the texture – is it smooth or rough? What shapes can you see? Is it smooth edged or rough?

3. Then lift the chocolate button to your nose and smell it for a while. What smells do you notice? Is it strong? Sweet? Does it remind you of anything?

4. Feel the chocolate button in your fingers. What can you feel? Is it solid or starting to melt? Does it feel rough or smooth? Notice the weight. Is it warm or cool?

Try to be aware of any thoughts you might have about the chocolate button, noticing any thoughts or feelings of like/dislike.

5. Bring the chocolate button to your lips and notice any changes in your body. Put the chocolate button in your mouth and let it start to melt on your tongue. How does this feel? What do you notice? What does it taste like? Does the taste change or stay the same?

6. Eat the chocolate button.

What did you notice during this exercise? Was it different from what you expected? Did you notice anything about the chocolate button that you have not noticed before?

This exercise shows how we can often do things without really thinking about them. It's as if we are half asleep or on "autopilot", rather than being fully aware in the current moment.

For example, we might eat a full bag of chocolate buttons without really tasting them. Or we might walk down the road with our minds focused on what we're having for tea, on college or on an argument that we've had with our friends, rather than our minds being focused on what it feels like in our bodies to be walking, the colours that we can see, the breeze on our skin, the crunch of the leaves under our feet.

Mindfulness is about choosing to bring our attention to our senses – what we can see, feel, smell, taste and hear in the present moment.

Here's a little exercise that helps us to do this:

Mindfulness exercise 2: Being aware in the present moment

Take a few minutes to ground yourself in the present moment. What is happening to your body and the world around you?

What can you see? Colours? Shapes? For example, trees, wildlife.

What can you hear? For example, people talking, traffic, birds.

What can you smell? For example, fresh washing, food, someone's perfume.

What can you taste? For example, food you have eaten, a mint.

What can you feel? For example, clothes against your skin, wind on your face, feet against the ground.

Are there any sensations in your body? Is it hot or cold?

You might also choose to mindfully observe an object – noticing what it looks like, smells like and feels like. Some examples of what you could use are:

- pebbles – sight, feel

- piece of material – feel, sight

- body lotion – feel, smell

- candle/fire – sight.

Personal experience – Sue

I carry a small pebble around. It's deep blue, and it turns an emerald colour when you hold it up to the light. It has a beautiful, natural pattern on it that reminds me of Japanese cherry tree blossom. It's smooth apart from a couple of small chips on one side that are rough when you run your fingers across them. When I'm feeling overwhelmed, I mindfully observe the pebble, which helps me to feel much calmer.

Another exercise to help you to focus your attention is the mindful blowing of bubbles.

Mindfulness exercise 3: Mindfully blowing bubbles

To do this, find some bubble solution. Slowly blow bubbles, noticing what it feels like to blow air carefully out of your mouth. Concentrate fully on the creation of the bubble. Watch the colours and what you can see on the surface of the bubble, including any light or reflections. Notice when they bump into each other. Look at the size and texture of the bubbles. Watch them pop! Be aware of any thoughts or feelings that you have during the exercise. Notice, but do not act on, any urges you may have to pop the bubbles (I know it's tempting!). Keep bringing your attention back to the feeling of blowing the bubbles and what you can see. Watch the bubbles floating around the room.

One of the most common mindfulness exercises is mindful breathing. This can particularly help with anxiety, as it helps to slow your breathing and calm it down.

Mindfulness exercise 4: Mindful breathing

1. Get into a comfortable position lying on your back or sitting. If you are sitting, keep your back straight and let your shoulders slowly drop. Make sure that you feel comfortable.

2. Feel your eyelids become heavy and gently close your eyes if it feels comfortable. If not, lightly rest your gaze on a point in the room and retain a soft focus.

3. Bring your attention to your breathing, breathing in slowly … and out slowly.

4. Now bring your attention to your stomach, feeling it rise gently as you breathe in and fall as you breathe out.

   Keep the focus on your breathing, being with each in-breath and with each out-breath.

5. Now bring your attention to your nose. Feel the cold air rushing through your nostrils when you breathe in, and the warm air rushing out through your mouth when you breathe out. If you find it hard to focus,

maybe swap things around, breathing in through your mouth and out through your nose.

6. Every time you notice that your mind has wandered off the breath, notice what it was that took you away. Then gently and compassionately bring your attention back to the feeling of the breath coming in and out of your body. Don't judge the thought or yourself, just let it be.

   If your mind wanders away from the breath many times, then your job is simply to gently bring your attention back to the breath every time.

   Practise this exercise daily. See how it feels to spend some time each day just being with your breath without having to do anything.

What to do with your anxious thoughts

Two of the main things that can get in the way of doing mindfulness are distractions and thoughts.

Everyone has unhelpful or difficult thoughts at times. When these thoughts start to build up, they can make you feel stressed or out of control, like the world is on your shoulders or your head is going to explode! Sometimes people want to push the unhelpful thoughts away and might try to block them out or ignore them.

This doesn't work. For example, if you try to block out a thought about a pink elephant (try it for 30 seconds) … what happens?

You will start to think about pink elephants even more!

Other people may try to focus on the thoughts, but this can lead to over-thinking and spirals of negative thoughts –

worrying about worrying (see Chapters 4 and 5 for more information on this).

Sometimes it can be useful to clear your mind of worries about the past and thoughts about the future. This can help you to feel more in control and calmer.

The important thing to remember is that our thoughts and worries are *just* thoughts and worries – they're not facts. We do not need to act on our thoughts and we can choose to just notice them. If we can notice and accept our thoughts, then we can just "let them be" – not trying to control them, but just noticing that they are there.

It can be helpful to imagine thoughts blowing away in the wind, or being carried away in a stream. Exercise 5 imagines thoughts being like clouds passing us in the sky.

Mindfulness exercise 5: Clouds in the sky

1. Imagine that you are lying down in a field staring up at the sky. You are feeling warm and relaxed. You gently gaze up at the sky.

The sky is bright blue with fluffy white clouds. Now watch the clouds floating through the sky, as they move through your field of vision and away. Notice their shapes and colours as they gently float through the sky, away from you.

2. Now imagine that the clouds are your thoughts passing through your mind. As they float past you notice them, observe them, and watch them float away.

3. Stand back and observe your thoughts as they come into your mind, as if they were clouds.

Notice them as they arise, and let them blow past, and float away.

Do this with each thought that comes into your mind.

4. As you notice each of your thoughts, don't hang on to them. Just notice each one and let it float by. As you watch the thought float away, it loses its hold on you and becomes less powerful.

Some people prefer to think about thoughts being like leaves that are being blown away by the wind, or like bubbles floating away.

Some people like writing down their thoughts on a piece of paper and then scrunching up the paper and throwing it away (noticing your thoughts and then letting them go). In Chapter 5, we talked about the idea of writing them down on toilet paper and flushing them away. This can be particularly useful at bedtime – letting go of the thoughts of the day, and allowing your mind to be at rest. It's also helpful at times when you feel overwhelmed with too much going on in your head.

Mindfulness of anxious feelings in the body

In a similar way to managing anxious thoughts, we can learn to notice, allow and accept anxious feelings in the body. Some people call this "riding the waves" of anxious feelings. What we know is that anxious feelings start to run out of fuel when we wait long enough, so we can accept them and wait for them to pass. When we experience these feelings, it can be useful to explore them in a mindful way. Step back and observe the feelings as you experience them in your body. Where can you feel them? (In your arms, face, heart area, legs?) What are the sensations like? How intense are the sensations? What shape are they? Do they come and go or stay the same? Stay curious and investigate what you are experiencing. Then it can be useful to take a few deep breaths and allow the sensations to "just be". Don't fight against them, or struggle with them, just allow them and wait for them to pass. Remind yourself that these are normal, bodily reactions and make peace with them.

This mindfulness of feelings can be difficult, particularly at first. But when you have managed to ride the wave of anxious feelings once or twice, and have watched them eventually stop, it can build up your confidence to be able to ride the wave again.

Obstacles you may face

People often feel that they are not doing the exercises right or that they should be able to focus better. Part of mindfulness is being able to notice that these thoughts are OK, and it's OK to take time to do the exercises. It does not matter how many times your mind wanders, just gently bring your attention back to the here and now.

How to put mindfulness into your everyday life (some ideas)

- When you wake up in the morning, gently bring your attention to your breathing. Mindfully notice five breaths just as they are (nothing fancy!).

- Bring your attention to your feet and toes – notice the warmth, the feeling of your socks, the pressure on different parts of your feet, the weight of your body and the feeling of balance over your feet. Maybe wiggle your toes.

- Find an object that's personal to you (e.g. a pebble/some jewellery). Carry it with you, using it at times when you are feeling anxious.

- Choose a mindful saying that's helpful to you – a mantra if you like. Write it or print it somewhere where you will see it regularly (e.g. put it on a card in your wallet, or stick it onto your mirror or bedside table). When you are feeling anxious, focus on the saying.

Personal experience – Phoebe

My mantra is: Focus on what's around you. Things happen how they happen. This is now.

- Mindfully look at an object. For example, you might choose a ceiling tile at the dentist's, or a pen or the patterns on a desk during an exam.

- If you're feeling tense, try a mindful body scan (see Exercise 6 below).

- When you're in the shower, bring your attention to the sensation of the water on your skin. How does it feel? Looking at the water, what can you see? You could think about the temperature – is it hot or cold? Notice the smell of any soaps you are using.

- When you're having a (bubble) bath, let your body relax and sink down into the bath, feeling heavy. How does your body feel? Watch the water and bubbles – what can you see? Colours? Shapes? Smells?

- When you're standing outside, take a moment to step back and mindfully notice what is happening around you. What can you see or hear? Then mindfully notice what is happening in your body. How does it feel? Can you feel the wind/sun on your skin?

- When you're feeling anxious, take five mindful breaths and bring your attention to your breathing. Every time your mind wanders to an unhelpful thought, gently bring your attention back to your breathing.

- When you are having unhelpful thoughts, bring your attention to an object (such as a picture, pen or photo). Mindfully look at the object, noticing what you can see and how it feels. When your mind wanders, gently bring your attention back to the object.

A final mindful exercise is the mindful body scan. This can particularly help you to relax your mind in the mornings or evenings. It may need a little more practice though. You can take as long as you wish to do this exercise. Some people like to set an alarm (you can even use mindfulness bells) to end the exercise, so that their thoughts are not focused on what they are doing next.

Mindfulness exercise 6: Body scan

1. Find a time and space where you are unlikely to be disturbed, where you can relax. Either sit down (keeping a straight back), or lie down on the floor. Relax into the chair, floor or cushion. Feel yourself sinking down, your arms getting heavy, your legs sinking down into the chair/floor. Let your shoulders relax. Feel your eyelids become heavy and gently close your eyes, if you feel comfortable doing this. Or just allow your eyes to gently focus on a point in the room.

2. Start by bringing your attention to your breathing. Breathing in … and out … noticing the rise and fall of your chest as you do so.

3. Then, when you are ready, imagine a spotlight shining on a part of your body, helping you to bring your attention and focus to that area. First, notice the spotlight move to your legs and feet. Notice any tension in your legs and feet, and as you breathe out feel the tension releasing out of your body, down through your legs, your ankles, your feet and down through the ground.

4. When you are ready, notice the spotlight move to the trunk of your body – your shoulders, your back, your stomach and your hips. Notice any tension in these areas, then as you breathe out, feel the tension releasing out of your body, down through the trunk of your body, your legs, feet and down through the ground.

5. Then notice the spotlight move to your shoulders, arms, and hands. Notice any tension, and then as you breathe out, feel the tension releasing out of your body, up through your arms, through the trunk of your body, down through your legs and feet and down through the ground.

6. Finally, notice the spotlight move to your head, face and neck. Notice any tension in these areas, and then as you breathe out, feel the tension releasing out of your body, down through your shoulders, the trunk of your body, through your legs and feet and down through the ground.

7. When you are ready, gently bring your attention back to your breathing. Feel the spotlight bringing a focus to the whole body. As you breathe in, notice any areas of tension, and as you breathe out, let them release and the tension flow out of the body.

8. When you feel ready, wiggle your toes, and gently come back to the room, ready and refreshed to carry on with your day.

✎7✎

Soothing Your Threat System

When we are feeling anxious or worried, we feel under threat and that leads to our threat system being activated. As we learned in Chapter 1, when our threat system is active, we are on hyper-alert and ready for flight, fight or freeze. Threat hormones are pumping around our body and preparing us to react. This might mean that our heart is racing, we are breathing very quickly, our body is tense, our stomach is doing flip-flops and we feel on edge. It is likely that our thoughts also feel like they are spiralling out of control!

Although this bodily reaction is designed to keep us safe and help us to survive any potential threat, the reaction in itself can be enough to make us feel panicky and even more anxious. We noticed in Chapter 3 that our thoughts, feelings, bodily sensations and behaviours are linked. So, when our heart is racing, or we are breathing quickly, this can lead to us having anxious thoughts and behaving in anxious ways.

Personal experience – Sue

I sometimes used to feel panicky when I was in crowds of people. I would breathe quickly, my head would feel dizzy and I would need to sit down – this would make me worry even more!

One of the best ways to calm down our threat system is to soothe ourselves. This helps us to slow down our bodily reactions, so that they are not reinforcing our feelings of anxiety. By altering these bodily reactions, this in turn impacts on our thoughts, helping us to feel much calmer overall. A calm body = a calm mind.

When we are young children and we face a challenge or difficulty that causes us distress, we are comforted or soothed by other people (usually a parent or carer), for example by hugs or calming words. This soothing then quickly brings down our level of distress (calms our threat system) and we feel safe and relaxed again. As we grow older, we start to learn ways to soothe ourselves, so that we don't always need to rely on others for that support (although seeking support from others is still important and talking to them or having a hug still works).

Although soothing can be a useful strategy, it is important to make sure that it is not getting in the way of you doing other things (you will need to challenge yourself too). For example, it would not be helpful to snuggle up in bed eating chocolate for a full week, avoiding what is making you anxious (although this might sound like a nice thing to do!). However, it can be a really helpful way of calming your threat system and dealing with anxious feelings in the moment. We cannot do any useful problem solving until we have got our thinking brain back online, so we nearly always need to soothe ourselves and feel calm before we can engage in other ways of managing worry or anxiety-provoking situations.

This chapter will outline several different ways to soothe your threat system: soothing using the senses, relaxation, breathing exercises and imagery. Different techniques will work for different people, so perhaps try some of these out and see which ones work for you (or make your own up!). It can also be helpful to try some of these out with someone else – perhaps a friend or family member, especially someone who can help you to use these strategies when you are feeling anxious. Getting someone else whom you trust involved can help you to feel even more soothed and safe, and they might enjoy it too!

Some ideas for soothing yourself are:

- Wrap yourself up in a comfy, warm blanket.

- Have a nice, relaxing bubble bath with candles.

- Choose your favourite hot drink and have it in a big mug (if you like hot chocolate, you could even add marshmallows).

- Listen to some relaxing music or sounds.

- Put on a large dressing gown or clothes that you can relax in (such as big, baggy clothes).

- Hide under your duvet for a bit.

What do you notice in your body when you try to soothe yourself? What happens to your thoughts?

You might notice a feeling of your body "slowing down" and relaxing, and your thoughts becoming more still.

Now let's explore how you can soothe yourself using the different senses.

Soothing using the senses

When you pay attention to your senses (in the present moment – see the information about mindfulness in Chapter 6), rather than the "noise" in your head, this can help you to feel calmer. This section lists some ideas for using each sense to soothe. Perhaps explore which ones work best for you.

Sounds

Some people like listening to soothing sounds such as the sound of a waterfall, a babbling brook, the waves in the sea crashing, birds tweeting, rustling leaves, rainforest sounds or the sound of rain.

You might also like listening to relaxing music or songs (with or without words). Some people like listening to beautiful or soothing music; others might prefer exciting or happy music (maybe make a playlist of your favourite tracks). Listening mindfully may also help (see Chapter 6). Alternatively, you might want to use audio recordings of guided mindfulness or relaxation exercises.

Touch

You may like to touch things that are silky and smooth, or soft and comfortable (such as fleece), or even things with a rough or abrasive texture. You might have a scarf, hat or gloves that feel soothing to the touch that you can wear, or take out of the house with you. Some people enjoy snuggling under a blanket or heavy duvet (or making a duvet fort). Having a hug from someone you care about can be quite soothing or you may just want to hold their hand. You might also choose to hug a cuddly toy or pillow.

Some people enjoy the sensation of putting body lotion on their skin, which can be even more sensory if it has a nice smell, or using a foot soak. Alternatively, body scrubs can give a stronger sensation on the skin and may feel tingly after (although don't scrub too hard!). It may be useful to find out whether you feel more soothed when feeling warm or cold; everyone is different. If you like the warmth, then wrapping up, a warm bath or shower, fluffy socks, or a hot water bottle might be pleasurable. But, if you prefer the cold, you may enjoy a cold flannel on your face, running your hands under cold water or a cold glass of water or drink with ice in it. Using cold items can sometimes help to counteract the warmth you may feel when anxious, from your racing heart and tensed muscles.

Sometimes, being able to get rid of some tension in your body through using items can help. For example, lots of people use Play-Doh or putty that they can squash, roll into balls, or throw as a way of reducing tension. There are also stress balls, or other foam balls, punch bags, or even punching a pillow.

Smells

What is your favourite smell? Does it help you to feel calm or relaxed? Smells trigger different feelings in people, so it can be useful to work out which ones help you to feel soothed. Some common soothing smells are freshly cut grass, peppermint, lavender and talcum powder. Some people might like the smell of baking or old books. You might have a favourite scent or perfume that you wear, or a scented candle or air freshener for your room. You may also choose to use scented body lotion, bubble bath or shower gel. There are ways of taking soothing smells with you wherever you go including wearing a scent, spraying the scent on something that you carry with you, or having some in a little container.

Sight

Which things do you feel are soothing to look at? You might feel soothed by watching a candle, spending time outside in a field, or near to water (e.g. a beach) and watching the waves crash onto the shore. You may enjoy watching the clouds float past in the sky. You might feel soothed looking at flowers or plants, so find ways to have these around you if you do. You might like things that remind you of positive, soothing memories such as photographs of family, friends, pets, your favourite sports team or musician, or times when you have felt content such as holidays. There might be objects that mean something to you, such as a particular piece of jewellery or watch, a certificate that you have won, a leaver's book or card that someone has written, or a special present that someone gave to you. Lots of people have special quotes, positive sayings, mantras or song lyrics that they like (see Chapter 4 for examples of positive coping statements) – you might want to write these out, or print them, and carry them with you (or keep them on your phone). You might have a favourite DVD or book that makes you feel soothed or brighter in mood.

Tastes and textures

When thinking about food and drink, both the taste and texture can be soothing. People's tastes can vary greatly, so again it is about exploring what makes you personally feel soothed. You might enjoy the tastes of food such as chocolate, fruit, hot toast, the comfort of having a warm drink such as tea or coffee. You may prefer the sensations of foods such as popping candy or sour sweets, which can help to focus your attention on something other than your thoughts (it's really hard to focus on anything else when there are mini-explosions or a sharp sourness in your mouth). There might be foods that remind you of soothing times, such as chicken soup (for times that you have been looked after), creamy mashed potato or ice-cream. Or foods that make you just feel happy when you are eating them – someone once told

Sue that however bad they were feeling, they could not help but smile when they were eating jelly. When you are feeling rubbish or anxious, it can often be difficult to find the motivation to go out to the shop to get these things, so it may be helpful to make sure that you have access to some soothing food items in your house. For example, you may choose to keep a sachet of your favourite hot drink or a special treat food (e.g. small bar of chocolate) nearby.

Whatever it is you find soothing, the important thing is to have it available and easy to access at times when you might be feeling anxious. You might choose to have a fluffy blanket in your room, a supply of special hot chocolate for times you are feeling anxious or a playlist of your favourite soothing music on your phone – whatever works for you.

Another way that people might make their soothing items easily available is by creating a self-soothe box…

Putting together a self-soothe box

A self-soothe box can be a very personal thing as it is unique to you, so the ideas below are just suggestions to get you started. Some people don't like the name self-soothe and prefer "happy box" or "self-care box".

You will need:

- a shoebox or decorative box

- paints/paper/glue/craft paper to decorate box (whatever you fancy)

- sensory items that you find soothing

- some of your favourite, comforting things.

Simply decorate the box as you wish (perhaps design it yourself so that it is particularly appealing to you) and use it to collect and store things that you can use to self-soothe. Put the box somewhere that you can easily find it, so that you can open it up and use the things inside it when you are feeling anxious. You might want to write notes to yourself, so that you can read them when you are feeling worried. You might want to include photographs or nice memories. You can include anything that is going to help you to feel soothed.

Personal experience – Phoebe

My self-soothe box contains:

☆ my mindfulness pebble

☆ my 'reasons to get better' book

☆ a book of good memories my friend made for me

☆ a teddy (Eeyore) from when I went to Disneyland – it reminds me of good things from the past

☆ Play-Doh to play with (and throw at walls when I feel frustrated)

☆ things to care for myself – hand cream and a face mask

☆ a little notebook to write down how I'm feeling

☆ reminders of things I want to do and places I want to go (Paris and Japan)

☆ some origami by my friend

☆ a word search book

☆ a funny book about Adventure Time that always cheers me up!

Relaxation and breathing

When you begin to feel anxious, your body becomes alert and tense and your breathing quickens. This, in turn, leads to your body speeding up which can prolong the feeling of anxiety and lead to further anxious thoughts. So, one way to address this and break the cycle is to learn how to relax your body and mind and slow down your breathing. The following exercises will focus upon muscle relaxation and slowing down your breathing.

Relaxing your body – muscle relaxation

During this exercise, we are going to tense, then relax, each set of muscles in turn. The aim of this is to release any tension, and give you a deeper sense of relaxation.

Exercise 1: Muscle relaxation

1. Lie on your back, as flat as possible, with your arms at your sides. Tense your facial muscles, screwing up your face, for a count of six. Then as you breathe out, let go of any tension and relax.

2. Tense the muscles in your shoulders, bringing them up to your ears, for a count of six. Then as you breathe out, let go of any tension and relax.

3. Tense your arm muscles, and clench each hand into a fist, for a count of six. Then as you breathe out, relax.

4. Tense your back muscles, bringing your shoulder blades downwards, for a count of six. Then as you breathe out, relax.

5. Tense the muscles in your stomach, for a count of six. Then as you breathe out, relax.

6. Tense the muscles in your bottom, for a count of six. Then as you breathe out, relax.

7. Tense the muscles at the top of your legs, your thighs and knees, for a count of six. Then as you breathe out, relax.

8. Tense the muscles in your lower legs, your calves and ankles, for a count of six. Then as you breathe out, relax.

9. Tense the muscles in your feet, curling your toes upwards, for a count of six. Then as you breathe out, relax.

Relaxing your breathing – slowing it down carefully

The average number of breaths per minute when you are relaxed is about 15–20 for a young person aged 15 years, and 12–20 breaths per minute for an adult. However, a person who is feeling anxious may take many more breaths per minute and may take bigger breaths too.

This means that more oxygen rushes to the brain which can lead to you feeling dizzy and faint.

Maybe have a go at measuring your breathing rate per minute both when you are relaxed, and when you are feeling anxious, and notice the difference.

My breathing rate when I am relaxed:

My breathing rate when I am anxious:

One way of helping us to feel calmer is therefore to gently slow down our breathing to a lower rate, restoring us to a more normal breathing pattern. Maybe try out the exercise below which can help you to focus on your breathing and start to gently slow it (also see Chapter 6 for a mindfulness breathing exercise).

Exercise 2: Breathing

1. Sit or lie down comfortably.

2. Close your eyes if you can, or choose a spot in the room to focus your gaze on gently.

3. Place one or both of your hands on your stomach (if using both hands, you can interlock your fingers).

4. Breathe in slowly, and notice your stomach and hand rise with your breath. Then slowly breathe out, again noticing your hand lowering as your stomach lowers.

5. Notice the pace of your breathing, and the rise and fall of your stomach and gently slow it down, allowing it to be slower and deeper, until it feels comforting and soothing.

Everyone has a slightly different breathing pattern that feels soothing to them, so play about with yours a little until you find one that helps you to feel relaxed and comfortable.

Relaxing and soothing the mind: imagery

Imagery can be very powerful in helping to calm down the parts of our brain involved in the threat system. There are lots of types of imagery that we can do, but here are just a couple of exercises that you can try out.

When doing the exercises below, find somewhere to sit or lie down where you are unlikely to be disturbed. The more you practise when you are feeling calm or things are still, the easier it will be to use these exercises when you are starting to struggle. It can be useful to have a trusted person helping you to do these exercises, perhaps reading out the scripts to you or helping you to build upon the images that you create.

Also, the image might not come for you straight away, or it might come and go, or change over time. All of these are absolutely fine … sometimes you might get a colour or shape or sound and this might be enough. It is just about bringing to mind whatever is soothing to you.

Safe place

When feeling anxious, it can sometimes be nice to go away in your mind to a calmer, more peaceful place. Often people choose to imagine a beach, field or floating in the sea. However, it is important to find somewhere that feels calming and relaxing to you.

In this imagery exercise, just allow a safe place to gently emerge from your mind, and see what appears.

Exercise 3: Safe place

1. Gently close your eyes and relax your body. Allow your breathing to slow down to a comfortable pace, with any tension flowing out of your body on each out-breath. When you feel ready, take a few steps forward in your mind, walking slowly into your safe place.

2. Imagine a space that feels safe and soothing to you. It could be something from a memory, or something completely made up. Just allow feelings of safety and calmness to flow around you. Imagine yourself feeling calm, relaxed, safe and soothed in this space.

3. Look around you – what does your safe place look like? What kind of colours, shapes, textures are there?

   What smells do you notice? Freshly cut grass? Baking? The saltiness of the sea?

   What can you feel? The hard ground underneath you? The sand beneath your toes? The sun on your face?

   You might be drawn to a field with long grass with the sun beating down on your face and a bright blue sky. Or you might be in a den made full of cushions and duvets. Or perhaps lying back floating in the sea. Or outside in a beautiful winter wonderland. Or snuggled up in front of a roaring fire, with a fluffy dog sat on your feet and the smell of cookies baking in the oven.

4. Allow these sights to come and go naturally in your mind, but stay with the feeling of safeness and calmness.

5. When you feel ready, allow yourself to slowly walk out of your safe place and back into the room. You might want to wiggle your toes to slowly bring you back.

Now that you have started to discover what your safe place might look like, it can help to practise this and build upon it. You might want to think about the questions above and start to write down a description of what can help you feel safe and soothed, or you might want to draw pictures or find photographs from the internet.

Personal experience – Sue

My safe imagery place is a beach in Wales – it's not exactly the same as the real beach, but has some of the same features. I love that it is so peaceful and quiet, it is quite remote and cut off. But my favourite bit has to be walking along the sand and paddling in the sea, listening to the waves breaking against the shore. Whenever I go to the beach (both in real life and in my imagination) it helps me to feel so calm and free, with a clear mind. So I recorded the sound of the waves from the beach on my phone so that I can use it to help me to find my safe place when I am struggling.

Soothing other

This second imagery exercise focuses upon the creation of a soothing, compassionate and comforting 'other' – this can be either a person, an animal or an object. The important thing is that this 'other' wants to support, comfort and be kind to you. Again, this 'other' may change over time and that is OK. This imagery can be useful when tackling difficult thoughts (see Chapter 4), where you can imagine what your soothing other would say to you, to help you to find an alternative helpful thought.

Exercise 4: Soothing other

1. Gently close your eyes and relax your body. Allow your breathing to slow down to a comfortable pace, with any tension flowing out of your body on each out-breath.

2. When you feel ready, imagine a soothing being moving towards you. Imagine that they know about the pain that you are feeling and that they deeply understand. Feel that they want to help you to feel soothed and comforted. Allow them to take shape as they start to approach you.

   What does your soothing other look like? Are they tall or small? Male or female? Old or young? A person, animal or object? Fluffy or smooth? How do they approach you? Do they walk, skip?

3. How does your other try to soothe you? Do they look in your eyes? Give you a hug? Hold your hands?

Do they talk to you? What is their voice like? Is it gruff or smooth? Loud or soft? What do they say to help you to feel soothed and comforted?

Allow these sights to come and go naturally in your mind, but stay with the feeling of safeness and calmness.

4. When you feel ready, allow yourself to come back into the room. You might want to wiggle your toes to slowly bring you back.

All soothed out

With this chapter, it can be useful to try out the different strategies and practise them when you are feeling calmer. It may be helpful to practise them with someone close to you, such as a parent or friend. You can find out which ones work for you and perhaps think about when you might be able to use them. These strategies will also be useful when putting together your Anxiety Survival Plan (Chapter 13).

$\gtrless 8 \lessgtr$

Getting a Good Night's Sleep

Sleep is so, so important for your mental health. If you struggle to sleep, this can lead to an increase in anxiety and worry, cause you to feel moody or irritable, or slow down your thinking processes. We also know that when people feel anxious or are worrying about something, this can stop them from sleeping properly. So it's like a never-ending cycle.

This chapter, therefore, has tips on how to get a good night's sleep, including how to cope with anxious thoughts around night-time.

Why is sleep important?

Although sleep might seem like a time when your body is relaxed and slowed down, or even switched off, this is definitely not the case. During sleep, your body is highly active, undertaking processes that are essential for your body and mind to function properly. Lots of physical processes happen when we sleep including our muscles recovering from exertion during the day and some important hormones (such as the growth hormone) being produced. So sleep even helps us to grow! It also helps us to process our emotions from the day, so a lack of sleep can lead to poor psychological wellbeing. We might also notice ourselves feeling overly anxious or giddy. It seems as if the brain knows that we are lacking in energy, so it gives us a rush of emotions so that we can cope with our daily life.

Sleep also helps us to cope mentally – without it, we can struggle to concentrate during the day, we might forget things, or feel disoriented or even confused. Research has suggested that the process of sleep is essential for our brains to naturally reset, which helps us to remember things and learn. Without a good night's sleep, we can therefore struggle physically, emotionally and mentally.

What is a healthy amount of sleep?

The amount of sleep needed for a healthy life changes as you grow older. Also, everyone is a bit different. Some people might be typically longer sleepers and some shorter sleepers. However, the average sleep 'requirements' are as follows:

- Age 5 to 13 years – approximately 9 to 11 hours per night

- Age 13 to 18 years – approximately 8 to 10 hours per night

- Age 18 and older – approximately 7 to 9 hours per night, but this reduces slightly in later life.

Your sleeping patterns

First, let's think a bit more about your sleep and where you might get stuck. If you understand more about your own sleeping patterns, such as the quality as well as quantity of your sleep, it can help you to think about what might improve it. It might also be useful to show your answers to someone close to you, to see if they can identify where you might be struggling.

Most nights ...

What time do you start your bedtime routine (e.g. putting pyjamas on, brushing teeth)?

What do you do between your bedtime routine and sleep (e.g. check phone, watch TV)?

What time do you usually go to bed?

How long is it generally before you go to sleep?

How many times do you wake up in the night?

How long are you usually awake for?

How much sleep, in total, do you get on an average night?

How many nights of the week do you struggle with your sleep?

How would you describe your sleep?

Do you feel refreshed after a night's sleep or still tired?

During the day ...

Do you still feel tired?

Do you struggle to concentrate?

Do you feel moody?

What impact do your sleeping patterns have on your life?

What would be better if you could sleep more?

What have you already tried to get a better night's sleep?

What makes it more difficult to sleep?

At the end of this chapter there is a sleep chart. If you complete this chart every day for a week, it will help you to be able to monitor and better understand your sleeping patterns.

Anxiety and sleep

We know that anxiety can have a big impact on sleep, and sleep can also have a big impact on anxiety, as discussed earlier in the chapter. But also, sometimes people are anxious about sleep itself, such as worries about whether they will ever get to sleep, worries about having a night when they are awake (again!), or worries about the impact of not sleeping on the day ahead. Feeling this level of anxiety, rather than relaxation, can interrupt a person's bedtime routine and make it much more difficult for them to fall asleep in the first place. So, the next part of this chapter will focus on ways to relax around bedtimes, get into a routine, and deal with any arising anxious thoughts.

Six ways to get a good night's sleep

This section outlines six different ways to improve your sleeping patterns, including thinking about how to improve your bedtime routine, the environment that you sleep in, helping your body and mind to relax, avoiding things that are likely to keep you awake, minimising distractions and dealing with anxious thoughts. Perhaps try some of these out and see which ones work for you. You can monitor their impact if you wish, using the sleep chart at the end of this chapter.

1. Make your bedroom a sleep sanctuary

The place that you are sleeping in can have a massive impact on your ability to get to sleep and your quality of sleep. Some people can sleep pretty much anywhere, such as on a noisy train. But other people will struggle much more and might need a place where they can relax their body into a comfortable position, with limited distractions around them and little sensory input (such as noise or light).

In order to help you to feel comfortable, it can be useful to try to get the temperature right so that you are not too hot or cold. A cooler room with enough blankets to stay warm is generally best. A room that is too hot or one that is too cold can lead to us feeling restless while sleeping and waking up more frequently. Opening the window for a little while before going to sleep can help to circulate the air in the room and make the room feel less stuffy.

It can also help to reduce the light and sounds in the room. Some people like to just make their room as quiet as possible (e.g. closing the door, removing noisy items) or even wear ear plugs to block out noises that might disturb their sleep. Other people like listening to relaxing music or sounds as they are drifting off to sleep. It is also best to try to make your room as dark as possible (to a level that you are comfortable with) and that doesn't keep you awake, as too much light in the room can make it difficult to fall asleep. You could also use a sleep mask or black-out blinds to keep the light out.

2. Get a good routine

One of the best ways of training your body to sleep well is to get into a consistent routine and to go to bed and get up at more or less the same time every day. This gets your body used to the pattern, so it is ready for sleep when you go to bed. Although it can be really tempting to take a nap during the day, particularly if you have not slept much the night before, it is best not to. If you take naps in the day, this can further disrupt your sleeping patterns at night, making you not sleepy or tired, or not wanting to go to bed. Even if you had a bad night's sleep and are feeling super tired, it's important that you try your best to keep your daytime activities the same as you had planned.

It's also better to only try to sleep when you actually feel tired or sleepy, rather than spending too much time awake in bed. If you haven't been able to get to sleep after about 20 minutes or more, get up and do something calming or boring until you feel sleepy, then return to bed and try again (but if you can't fall asleep after about 20 minutes, then get up again … etc.).

You can also develop your own sleep rituals to try to remind your body that it is time to sleep – some people find it useful to do relaxation stretches or breathing exercises or have a cup of non-caffeinated tea before going to bed.

3. Things to avoid

When you are trying to relax your body and mind, in preparation for sleep, you are trying to slow down your thinking and bodily reactions. But some chemicals that we may take into our body will counteract this and lead to us being more awake, alert and hyper-active. These include caffeine, cigarettes and alcohol. So it's best to avoid these for at least four hours (if not more) before going to bed. Energy drinks should also be avoided wherever possible, as although they may make you feel less tired at the time, they may also prevent you from being able to get to sleep later on. If you exercise in the evenings, it's best to do this as early as possible so that you have time to switch off from this and relax your mind and body before going to bed. Some people really enjoy having a small supper before going to bed (mmm, toast!) and this can actually be helpful in promoting sleep. But it is usually best not to have a heavy meal in the late evening, so small snacks are better.

4. Minimising distractions

In order to relax your mind, it helps to attempt to shut off from everyday distractions and demands. We can train our minds to get ready for sleep by following a good sleep routine (see (2) 'Get a good routine' above), but sometimes this can be difficult if we are distracted by other things which can take up our focus and attention. Wherever possible, try not to use your bed for anything other than sleeping, so that your body starts to associate your bed with sleep. If you use your bed as a place to watch TV, eat or work on your laptop, then your body will not learn the bed–sleep connection.

One of the biggest things that stops most people (including us) from sleeping is looking at our phones. It can be so tempting to just check something on the internet, or see why it beeped, but this will bring your mind straight out of your sleep routine and back into the everyday world. Even worse than this, recent research has told us that spending more time looking at screens on devices (such as your phone) can lead to disrupted sleep, including poorer quality sleep and finding it takes longer to fall asleep. There is a biological reason for this, as there is a blue light that shines out of your phone (and other devices) which prevents a sleep hormone called melatonin being released. The level of this hormone usually increases a few hours before you go to sleep and is like a signal to the body to prepare you for sleep. So, when this hormone is not released, it will be far more difficult for you to fall asleep. Also, the lights behind the screens of devices can cause the brain to be more alert (tricking the brain into thinking that it is daytime), thus preventing us from sleeping even more. Although lots of us may end up going on our phones and looking through our social media accounts, this is likely to delay and interrupt our sleep routines. It will keep our minds busy and active and we might get drawn into a conversation or worry. So it's usually best to put our phones away from our beds (on silent) so that we cannot be distracted by them, and to avoid using any devices with screens for an hour or two before bedtime.

Another big distraction that people often talk about is watching the time. When you are struggling to sleep, it can be easy to keep checking the time to see how long it is since you last checked and how long until the morning. However, frequently checking the time during the night is likely to reinforce negative thoughts such as "It's so late, I can't sleep" or "I've only slept for four hours". These thoughts can then lead to an increase in anxiety and frustration, which in turn can lead you to be less likely to fall asleep. It can also have an even worse effect if you check the time on your phone (see above information about the screens of devices). So try to check the time less and only when you really need to.

Personal experience – Scott

I used to always check my phone at night and kept checking it whenever I got bored of trying to sleep. So now I turn off the Wi-Fi and keep my phone at the other side of the room. This means that it is a lot more effort for me to cross the room and check it, so I don't bother! I have been sleeping a bit better since.

5. Dealing with anxious thoughts

Worries and anxious thoughts can sometimes really get in the way of us falling asleep. We might have thoughts racing around our minds, or just one or two thoughts stuck in our head. As we learned in Chapter 3, these thoughts can also have an impact upon our bodily reactions making us physically feel anxious and tense, which can further affect our ability to relax and sleep. So, as well as relaxing our bodies, it can be useful to find a way to calm down our minds. Typically, when you are trying to go to sleep, it is best not to try out full thought challenging (as described in Chapter 4) as this can make your mind even more alert. But there might be some calming words or statements that you can use to gently bring your anxiety levels down. For example, you might say to yourself, "Everything is OK now, I can sort this in the morning" or you might want to focus on the words "relax" or "calm". Mindfulness exercises (Chapter 6) may also support you to calm your thoughts before attempting sleep, such as focusing on taking a few mindful breaths or mindfully having a shower or brushing your teeth (whilst allowing your thoughts to drift in and out of your mind in a non-judgemental, mindful way). Imagining your safe place (Chapter 7) or soothing other (Chapter 7) could also help you to soothe your mind and calm your thoughts, giving them a more specific focus.

If there are lots of thoughts or worries going around in your mind when you are trying to sleep, or you wake up with a particular worry or concern in your head, it might be useful to write these things down and then leave them aside when they come into your mind. You might do this before going to bed, so that you can then let go of the worries until the morning, so that they are not racing around in your mind when you are trying to sleep. (See Chapter 5 for more ideas for dealing with worries.)

Another way to deal with anxious thoughts that might arise in your mind at night is "thought blocking". This technique can be helpful to deal with worrying thoughts if you use it straight after you wake up, before you start to feel too wide awake. To do thought blocking, repeat the word "the" (or a similar, simple, boring word) every two seconds in your head with your eyes closed … don't say it out loud, but sometimes it can help to mouth it. Keep repeating the word for about five minutes (if you can). The idea of this is that your working memory can only hold a certain number of pieces of information at one time. Filling up your working memory with the word "the" leaves little space for you to think about other things. A very boring technique, but boring is good for sleep times!

6. Relax

Relaxing the body and slowing it down can really help us to feel sleepy and prepare our bodies to fall asleep. In order to feel more relaxed in your body, you may choose to do a breathing or relaxation exercise, or just gently let go of any tension in your body. Doing a progressive muscle relaxation exercise before going to bed (see Chapter 7) as part of your winding-down routine can also help the muscles in your body to relax. Some people enjoy bubble baths or showers as part of their night-time routine. If you choose to have a bath, it is best to have it one hour before bedtime so that your body temperature is not too high when you are trying to sleep. You might also want to use some nice-smelling bath bubbles or salts, or shower gel, to help you to relax. Having a warm, milky drink before going to bed can help people to fall sleep, but it is important to make sure that it hasn't got caffeine in it. Other people enjoy using smells to soothe them before bedtime and help them to feel relaxed. A common bedtime scent is lavender, but you can use whatever smells soothing to you (see Chapter 7).

	Sun	Mon	Tues	Wed	Thurs	Fri	Sat
Time I went to bed							
Approx. time I went to sleep							
Number of times I woke up							
Time I woke up in the morning							
Time I got up							
Describe my sleep (two words)							
Rating of sleep*							
What techniques I tried to improve my sleep							

*How I would rate my sleep (0–10 where 0 = awful, didn't sleep at all, and 10 = excellent, had good quality sleep for adequate amount of time)

Table 8.1 Sleep chart

9

School, College and Exam Stress

School or college is a large part of a person's life and it takes up so much time and thinking space. Even when you are away from school or college, you might be thinking about what you need to do, doing (or pretending to do) your homework, or thinking about upcoming exams or coursework. So, for young people, school or college can be a big source of anxiety and worry, both when you are there and when you are at home.

If you find school difficult, you won't be the only one. Even though other people might seem to be coping OK on the surface, many will be struggling underneath. You might think of it like a duck sitting on a pond. The duck may appear calm and serene gently gliding on the smooth surface of the water, but underneath the water, the duck's feet are frantically paddling!

You might also find that people talk about how much studying they are doing, or how well they are doing with a piece of coursework, which might make you feel quite panicky. One of the main things that can make people feel anxious at school is comparing themselves to other people and not feeling good enough. People may also feel under pressure to do well, worry that they have not done enough revision or study, worry about feeling like a failure, or be working towards a particularly challenging goal or grade and fear falling short of it. As with other things that might make you feel anxious, it can really help to talk to someone close to you, or someone who can help, about how you are feeling (see Chapter 11 which covers talking to people about your anxiety). This could include a friend, family member, pastoral support or a teacher whom you get on with. They might be able to give you some help or advice, or arrange for some additional support for you. Usually it is best to speak to someone about this as soon as possible, before the anxiety and work mounts up (but even later on, this can really help).

How does anxiety affect us at school or college?

Anxiety is part of our threat response (see Chapter 1), and it can significantly interfere with our thinking. It can make us focus solely on what we feel is the threat (e.g. not doing "well enough" or failing) and stop us from being able to do our work and focus or concentrate. It can lead us to make errors or forget what we were going to say or write. Although anxiety can be helpful in motivating us to revise and work hard (otherwise we might just spend time having fun when we should be learning algebra), we know that too much anxiety gets in the way of us being able to think clearly. This is especially important when it comes to doing well at school and college.

When our threat system is activated, all of our focus is narrowed onto the perceived threat. This means that we can struggle to think about anything other than the threat. So we might be thinking things such as, "Aargh, an exam! I've forgotten everything!" (which might lead to a spiral of anxious thoughts), rather than being able to recall how to say "hello" in French ... "Bonjour". So, it is important to notice when our threat system is activated, and learn to be able to soothe our threat system so that we can re-engage our thinking brain again. Chapter 7 focuses on techniques to soothe your threat system more generally, but this current chapter will give examples of how to do this, and calm our thoughts, specific to school or college settings.

Avoid avoidance!

A common way of trying to cope with anxiety is to avoid whatever is making you anxious (see Chapter 3 for more information). Sure, this works in the short term and can make you feel calmer for a little while as you are avoiding the potential threat that your mind has detected. We know that with schoolwork this can just lead to the unavoidable building up, then you end up with lots of pieces of work past the deadlines and last-minute cramming for exams! This in turn is likely to make you feel even more panicky and under threat; but it is impossible to avoid things forever. So it is good to face your worries head on (with a bit of support) and, where possible, plan in advance. This chapter therefore thinks about ways to address, rather than avoid, your anxiety triggers. It will go through top tips for studying and exams and how to make a study haven, to help you to get the best out of college or school and feel more prepared and less anxious.

Top tips for studying

These top tips focus on different study techniques that could be useful in coping with anxious thoughts. They aim to be proactive, to help you to feel prepared in your work and thus lessen the potential anxiety you feel. Maybe try some out and see which ones work for you.

- If you struggle to concentrate in lessons, see if you can record them (asking permission from your teacher first) so that you can play back and see anything that you have missed. Or see if there is any supporting multi-media that you can use to support your studies.

- Break your studies into small chunks. Your attention span will last up to 40 minutes, so it is often best to study for 30 minutes, then have a break for ten minutes. This is similar to the "Pomodoro" technique, which breaks up work into intervals. Maybe plan nice things to do in your breaks (little treats) such as having a drink, a small bite to eat, a walk outside, and a bigger treat for the end of your study session.

- You might like to write down all of the topics that you need to study and then tick them off when you complete each one.

- Make sure that the goals that you set are realistic – if you plan to study three different topics in a day, is that do-able, or is that just going to leave you feeling stressed and wanting to give up? If it's not do-able, just try to study two instead.

- Sometimes worry about work can stop you from actually working (see the avoidance section above). You might feel that you "just can't write anything" or don't know what to say. The best thing that you can do when you feel like this is to have a go. Even if you only manage to get a few words down, or a sentence memorised, it is better than nothing. You might choose to take a few minutes out to calm your threat system (see Chapter 7), then it can be good to just have a go.

- If you get stuck with lots of worrying thoughts in your head and cannot concentrate, take a few minutes out. Perhaps use some mindfulness (see Chapter 6), such as taking a few mindful breaths (focus upon the sensations in your body as your breaths come and go, noticing thoughts as they pass you by, but not clinging onto them). You might also want to take a few minutes away from your study area to have a proper break and calm and soothe your threat brain, before going back to your work.

- If these difficult thoughts persist, you might choose to do some thought challenging (see Chapter 4) to try to get an alternative perspective.

The problem with perfectionism

Being a perfectionist is widely thought to be a positive thing. The key problem with perfectionism is that nobody is actually perfect (although they might seem to be). People might be really good at something, or even really, really good at something, but everyone will make a mistake in the end. Some people may worry that if they don't get all top grades, then they are letting themselves or other people down or are a failure (see the section below about pressure). It can then feel like a massive blow, or that their world is crumbling down if they don't get the grades that they were hoping for. If we try to be perfect, then we are setting ourselves up to fail as no one can be perfect all of the time. All we can do is be "good enough", try our best and see what happens.

So, having realistic goals and aims is important, as is knowing that exams aren't everything, and that there are other options if we don't get the grades that we are hoping for. But the process of learning to fail, and knowing that you can survive and get over failure, is actually also a really important psychological skill to have. When someone has been through failure and come out of the other side, this can start to build a psychological resilience or strength in them – so that they know that they can fail things and still survive in the future and that it is not the end of the world.

With perfectionism often comes self-critical thinking. Phrases such as "I should have …" and "I could have …" are common. It can therefore be helpful to use your thought-challenging skills (see Chapter 4) to help you to think of some alternative, more compassionate, phrases that you can say to yourself if you notice yourself being critical. Asking yourself, "What would my best friend/parent say?" can help with this.

Make a study haven

One thing that can be important in helping you to be able to focus and concentrate on studying is to have somewhere that feels safe, calm, and away from distractions. This section therefore focuses on how to create an optimal learning environment within your home (and tips that you can take on the move). As most people don't have lots of space to choose from, and may have to share with other family members, this can be a real challenge. It might therefore be useful to explain to your family the importance of you having some quiet, dedicated study space around revision or homework times to help you to focus.

- Make sure that you plan some time in your diary to study – have it blocked out. You might want to make sure that you are going to have some peace and quiet in the house (where possible) and won't be disturbed.

- Some people prefer to study with music on or relaxing sounds. Others prefer quiet – see what works for you. You might like to create a study playlist with relaxing or motivating music or sounds.

- Make sure that you feel comfortable, but not so comfortable that you will be sleepy. Sitting up straight might help with this and prevent backache. Posture is really important, especially when using laptops as we tend to slump forwards.

- If you're lucky enough to have a desk then make sure that it is fairly tidy and de-cluttered (maybe tidy at the end of each study period?). If you don't have this, then find a space in the house where you can study, for example, a dining room table.

- You might need things to help you to study (or might just like buying stationery) like post-its, highlighters, dictionaries, flash cards. Try to buy these in advance of your study session and make sure that they are close by when you need them.

Personal experience – Bridie

I liked to study in the library as it meant there were no distractions and I could relax when I got home. I was also a big fan of lists and stationery to make me feel more in control when the workload of studying felt too much. I would make a detailed list of all my deadlines and the topics I needed to cover, then use post-its and cue cards to make sure all the most important points could be stuck on my wall. Whenever I had finished studying a topic or a deadline passed, I would cross it off on my list using a thick black marker pen – very cathartic! I always made sure that I had lots of treats to reward and calm myself when I needed it.

Make time for you

Although this chapter is focused primarily on tips to help you in the moment with your studies and exams, the thing that will help you the most in the longer term is generally looking after yourself. It is so important to care for your mind and your body, and when you do this, it has a positive knock-on effect on your overall physical and mental health, thus improving and lessening your anxiety and making you feel better overall. To look after yourself properly, it is important to get a good sleep routine and an adequate amount of sleep each day (see Chapter 8). Without enough sleep, your concentration, focus, ability to learn, and memory will be badly affected, as well as your mood. So, although pulling an all-night study session before an exam might seem like the best thing to do, it really isn't as it is likely to lead you to struggle to concentrate the following day (and you may forget what you learned that evening). Having a good night's sleep is more likely to do wonders for your focus and your mood the next day.

Other ways of looking after yourself include making sure that you have a healthy diet and do some regular exercise – both these have also been shown to have a positive impact upon anxiety levels. So avoid skipping meals and make sure that you have breaks and times slotted in for your everyday activities. You might also want to build breaks into your study timetable for activities that you enjoy, or those that relax you, such as going for a walk or talking to friends. These activities are likely to improve your mood in general and give you a break from the more intense study.

Top tips for exams

The following top tips focus on how best to prepare yourself for an exam, but also how to cope with anxiety if it comes to you during an exam:

- Try to get a good night's sleep the night before an exam. It can be difficult to sleep, especially if you are worried about the exam, but if you do manage to sleep this can be beneficial in terms of feeling calmer and more prepared, and helping you to focus and remember things on the day. See Chapter 8 for sleep tips.

- Although it might be tempting to have an energy drink (or other caffeine drink) before an exam, this increase in caffeine could actually increase feelings of anxiety and worry (both anxious thoughts and bodily reactions). So these energy drinks are best avoided for at least a few hours before an exam (or it's best not to drink them at all).

- You might like to have a little mantra or phrase that you can focus on, and say to yourself, before or during the exam such as "You can do it".

- If you are struggling in an exam, then take a moment to re-focus. Maybe take a few deep breaths and focus on your breathing (see Chapter 6 and 7 for breathing techniques).

- Perhaps use a mindfulness technique (see Chapter 6) to re-focus your attention. You might want to focus your attention onto your pen, or the patterns on the desk, and study them mindfully, bringing your attention gently back to the object when your mind wanders. After a few moments, when your head feels clearer, you can go back to the exam. If you plan to use this technique during an exam, it can be useful to practise it first.

- You also might want to play a short mindfulness game of studying the room and finding something in the room that you have not seen before, such as an air vent, or a pattern on the curtains (paying attention to your surroundings in the present moment, to focus the mind).

- Plan a fun activity to do after the exam, which can give you something to look forward to and focus on. This can also give you some helpful distraction after the exam, when there can be an overwhelming (unhelpful) temptation to look back through study notes to see what you have got wrong!

- It might be useful to spend some time in the exam hall before an exam. For example, perhaps go in and sit down a few days before, so that you start to get to know, and feel more comfortable in, the room. It might be useful to do a relaxation exercise or something soothing (see Chapter 7) whilst in the room, so that your brain can start to associate feelings of calmness with the room environment.

Support available at school and college

If, after trying out all the above, you are still feeling panicky about your study or upcoming exams, then it is important to let someone at your school or college know if you haven't done so already (see Chapter 11 for ideas about talking to people and accessing support). Sometimes schools have additional support in place for pupils who struggle with exams and they might be able to talk through options or ideas with you, or they might have a smaller room that you can use.

Pressure from others

Often when we feel pressure to do well at school or exams, some of this pressure might come from other people such as parents or teachers. We might feel that we "have" to do well to make them proud of us, or that they are expecting us to get high grades and will be disappointed in us if we don't. Sometimes their expectations may be unrealistic or highly challenging. This can feel like a whole load of pressure on top of any worries that we might already have about our exams! This pressure might also make us want to avoid talking about it with them, become angry or frustrated towards them, or increase our anxiety.

It can be helpful to have a talk with other people about what they are thinking that you will achieve in your study or exams. You can then say what you feel is realistic that you might achieve and how they can support you in working towards this. This openness can relieve pressure and encourage helpful communication. See Chapter 11 for information about talking to people about your anxiety. Please also see the Useful Information section at the end of the book for links to resources about school, college and exam stress.

❧ 10 ☙

Transitions

Transition and change is something that everyone must manage; nothing ever stays the same and adolescence is a time with more transitions than any other. Transitions can often be exciting and positive, but can also be difficult and challenging. When we talk about transitions, people often think about big or important changes; for example, moving schools, when parents separate or losing someone that we love. Transitions, however, are something we are managing more regularly than that; in fact, we manage them every single day. During a school or college day, you transition from one class to another. A parent might have to go on a work trip or fall ill, meaning that there is a change to the routine and who is with you at home. These are transitions too and for many of us they can be a source of stress and anxiety which may challenge or overwhelm our usual coping strategies and ways of taking care of ourselves.

EXAMPLES OF TRANSITIONS IN ADOLESCENCE

☆ moving class at school or college

☆ starting a new hobby or activity

☆ bereavement, someone we love dying

☆ getting a new teacher

☆ a parent getting a new job

☆ moving house

☆ emigrating to a new country

☆ the ending of an important friendship or relationship

☆ starting to do things on your own, for example travelling alone

☆ starting an intimate relationship with someone that you care about

☆ starting to earn your own money.

Even positive transitions can cause us to feel unsettled and anxious alongside the excitement and anticipation. These anxious feelings might be about the unknown or it could be because there is loss as well as new beginnings. A good example of this can be going to college or university. Often young people feel excited about going to college and starting a course that they have chosen, but feel very sad about leaving their friends and family behind and anxious about not knowing the building, their new classmates, or what the expectations of them in this new setting will be.

These feelings are typical and understandable, as humans don't always like change. Also, the loss of relationships through bereavement, moving away or relationship breakdowns are extremely painful. Mostly, difficult transitions feel strange and can be uncomfortable. It can be helpful to remind ourselves that transitions can also be a time of growth and an opportunity to learn about ourselves and develop new coping skills. There are ways that we can approach transitions, and all the feelings that might arise, which make these challenging periods in our lives easier to manage. If we feel we have some control then we might sometimes feel sad or uncomfortable, but we are also more likely to learn and grow from them. We can enlist the help of our family and friends too.

Prepare yourself

We do not always have the luxury of preparing for transitions. Some changes in our lives happen unexpectedly and then we have to deal with the consequences whilst dealing with the shock. Some transitions, however, we know are coming for months or even years. When we have time to prepare it can be helpful to make the most of this time. If we are feeling anxious and unsettled then it can be tempting to bury our head in the sand and pretend that it is not happening.

This ignoring and avoidance is normal and understandable, but is it helpful?

If we can accept a change is coming then we can prepare ourselves and begin to address any worries that we might have head on. If you are starting a new college and the open day or interview that you attended was last year, arrange another visit; even if it is just asking someone to drive you there so that you can see the building again. If it is moving to a new country or too far to drive, then even looking at photos will make the place more familiar and can reduce your anxiety. When you are feeling anxious about starting a new activity and meeting new people, then taking the time to plan your route and even practising it beforehand can be helpful for increasing your confidence. It is one less thing that will be "new" on the day. Solving the small worries makes you feel more capable and more able to face the new situation.

It is often a good idea to sit with someone you trust to talk about the upcoming change and identify any worries and possible problems so that you can start to make plans for exactly how you could manage them. You can use problem-solving techniques like the ones used in Chapter 5 to think about solutions to challenges and then to make plans and even practise what you might say in new or scary situations.

PROBLEM-SOLVING METHOD

☆ List all possible solutions (including silly/ impossible ones).

☆ Write down all the pros and cons (you can just do your top three if you want to keep it short).

☆ From this decide which is the best solution.

☆ Make a plan of how to carry this out including role play where necessary or helpful.

Structure and routine

When we are going through a change we can lose our usual daily routines. A lack of structure and neglecting these routines can make us feel even more out of control when things get stressful and can mean we are ignoring the basics of getting a good night's sleep and eating a balanced diet. Simple things like keeping your mealtimes and bedtimes regular and as close to your "normal" routine as possible is a good start and helps you to take care of yourself. It is important that you continue making time for yourself and the things that make you feel calm and relaxed.

If you are going through a big transition (like moving placements or leaving home for the first time), then you might be looking forward to leaving behind the old routines that were in place in your old home. In this case, it is worth spending some time thinking about what you want your new routine to look like and to include the things that will help you to relax and stay calm.

Make your peace

If you are leaving people behind and moving on to a new class or a new school, or you or your friend/family member is moving away, sometimes it seems easiest to let any differences be forgotten. Avoidance is often tempting when the alternative is a difficult conversation; however, if something has upset you or you feel that you might have upset someone else, it is important to make your peace and try to correct any misunderstandings. It might be an uncomfortable or difficult conversation, but if you can be brave then rather than taking the baggage with you, you can move on knowing that you did everything that you could to make it a good ending with no unresolved issues. Think about it as "exposure" to a feared situation and an opportunity to test out your predictions about what you think might happen, and also learn how well you can cope even when things don't go the way you would like (see Chapter 3).

Say your goodbyes

Saying goodbye and having a good ending is important in making a transition successful. Goodbyes can be sad and difficult but they can also be a time of celebration. It is a chance to let people know that they have been important to you and to make meaning from the end of a chapter in your life. If it is hard to tell someone face to face what they have meant to you, then writing a note or a card can be another way to do this.

Make sure that you plan your goodbyes with people or there is a danger you simply drift away. It might be that you plan a big party with lots of important people, or it might just be a quick coffee or walking home together. Take photos of important people before you go and make sure you offer ways to keep in touch. Plan a return visit or a reunion.

Sometimes goodbyes are a personal and individual process that is more about feeling OK with the ending than communicating with others. Be creative. Re-visit your favourite places, take photographs, make a collage or keep a journal.

Seek support

Let people know that you are struggling with a change or transition, don't assume that they know. We all need other people to help us when we are struggling. Your family might be going through the transition with you and have stresses of their own, or it might be that those around you have not realised that you have mixed feelings about a transition that on the face of it seems really exciting.

Sharing your worries can make problem solving easier as well as soothing your anxiety. If you are not someone who often asks for help then you might need to think about how you can do this. There are some ideas in Chapter 11 about talking to others about your fears and worries.

Give yourself some time

It is completely normal to feel anxious and unsettled (as well as excited) when we are approaching something new. When we have a big life change thrust upon us by the universe, then it can be terrifying and make us feel out of control. A loss like a parent leaving the family home or someone whom we love dying can feel devastating. It takes time. Human beings have an amazing capacity to adapt to new and strange situations, but it is normal to feel really terrible for a while and it takes time for us to get used to our new life. Be kind to yourself. Be aware of being self-critical and use the ideas from Chapters 6 and 7 to help you to be mindful, relax and soothe yourself through this difficult time.

TOP TIPS FOR MANAGING TRANSITIONS

1. Be prepared! Face your worries head on and when possible get familiar with what is to come.

2. Talk to people whom you trust about how you are feeling.

3. Keep your daily routines as "normal" as you can.

4. Say your goodbyes and heal old hurts wherever possible.

5. Be kind to yourself.

---

৯ 11 ৎ

Getting Extra Help

Talking to people about your anxiety

When you are struggling with your anxiety, it is important to tell someone close to you so that they can help you out and support you. Often this person is a parent, carer, sibling or grandparent but this extends to whoever you want it to be, including close friends or teachers. As you can see in the personal stories in Chapter 12, talking to people about their anxieties was often a positive turning point for many of the young people.

Telling someone you are struggling can make it feel like you are in a vulnerable position, which can be very scary! In our experience, we have found that after telling someone, we feel relieved. It has allowed people to help and understand why we might respond in the ways that we do.

We think, when talking to people, there are a few things you can do that can make it a little easier:

1. Find a place you feel comfortable in and meet the person there (e.g. a café or a park). Make sure it is somewhere where you feel safe and feel you can talk freely.

2. Create an idea in your head of what you want to say and how you are going to broach the subject but don't over-plan. If you think too much about it, it will cause you even more anxiety.

3. Only say what you feel comfortable saying; you are under no obligation to say more than feels OK. If the person begins to ask questions that you don't want to answer just simply say, 'I wanted to let you know I'm struggling but, at the moment, I don't feel ready to talk in detail about my anxiety' or something similar.

4. It's likely that when the person you have chosen finds out about your struggles they will want to help. Maybe have a think about the ways they could help you out (e.g. distraction, being someone you can contact when you're having a hard day etc.). Tell them these things.

5. Sometimes the best thing to do is to rip off the plaster and just do it. In our experience, the build-up is always much worse than the anxiety of actually doing the thing we're anxious about. Once you've said it and got over the initial rush of adrenaline, things seem easier and relief usually kicks in. Over-planning can make you feel very anxious and sometimes just going for it saves a lot of stress.

6. Talking to people can be scary but often they just want to help you. Admitting you are struggling and telling someone is a big step in overcoming your anxiety and often makes you feel more at ease with the person you have told.

Personal experience – David

I had to take a long hard look at myself and recognise that I needed support. I called my parents and told them how I was feeling and had a good cry over Skype, which actually made me feel amazing at the time! It felt like the entire one year's worth of anxiety just came flooding out in that conversation and it was such a release that I could physically feel my body relax ... I discussed everything that was going on for me with some of my closest friends, who had no idea I was struggling. These conversations with friends provided me with advice and support that actually made my situation and the decisions I had to make feel much less overwhelming... What I have realised more than anything from this period is that it is so important to share my concerns and ask for support at times when I feel worried or anxious.

Other ways to communicate

Sometimes it might feel too difficult to talk to people directly about your anxiety, so you might want to think about other ways to let people know. You might choose to write a note to someone close, such as a letter to tell a parent how you have been feeling, which you can hand to them. Or you might agree with a parent that you will let them know via text when you are struggling (even just sending them an emoji – as long as they will know what it means). Some people also make "communication cards" where they make small cards with pictures or words on to indicate different moods, which they can show to their parent or trusted adult to let them know how they are feeling. Whatever works best for you. Sometimes people say, "Well, they should know anyway, I've not been myself." In some ways, this guessing what other people might be thinking can be a bit like a mind-reading error (see Chapter 4), which could lead to us feeling frustrated with the other person or let down. Sadly, other people can't always pick up on signs when you are struggling, so we think it's always best to let them know directly.

What can get in the way

Often people can be fearful of the reactions of others, including worrying that they might be angry, sad, disappointed, shocked or upset. They might even worry about being a burden to the other person, especially if the other person is going through a difficult time themselves. This can then lead to the young person ending up keeping things to themselves even more and trying to cope alone – which we know isn't helpful. What we have found, from all of our work with families, is that although parents and trusted others might initially be surprised (although they usually aren't) or sad that their child is feeling that way, usually parents are really pleased that their child has built up the courage to tell them, so that they can give them support and comfort. Often parents might have noticed that their child is not quite themselves, or may be a bit more withdrawn, but have not known why. Sometimes the other person may not know quite how to respond initially, or what to say, but that is OK. If you have managed to let them know how you feel, then you can start to work at talking about it more together. It may also be helpful to share your Anxiety Survival Plan (see Chapter 13) to help them to better understand your anxiety and how they can support you.

Personal experience – Scott

When I first told my mum about my anxiety issues, I was a nervous wreck. I had been thinking about it for a long time and ended up sending a message to her on a particularly difficult morning. Later that night when we talked, it was scary, but after a few minutes I realised that it was a good thing to do and started to feel a lot less alone in my issues.

Support at school or college

If you are struggling with your anxiety at school or college, it might be useful to meet with a member of staff whom you have a good relationship with, for example, your form teacher, head of year, learning support or pastoral care.

Questions that you might want to ask include:

- Is there a place in school or college where I can go if I am struggling with my anxiety?

- Is there someone that I can talk to about this (e.g. counsellor/pastoral support)?

- Is there any additional help that I can get with my exam preparation? (You may need some special help in your exams.)

- Are you running any sessions on how to manage exam stress? Or is there anywhere that I can get some help with this?

See the Useful Information section at the end of the book for more information and resources.

Mental health services

If your anxiety is continuing to impact upon your everyday life or causing you lots of distress in specific situations, then we recommend that you go to see your GP. They can think with you about whether a referral to a mental health service might be helpful and can let you know more about what is available in your area. They may also suggest the use of medication (the Headmeds website in the Useful Information section can be helpful).

It can be scary going to mental health services for the first time, but the people who work in these services are very understanding and are not judgemental at all. Everyone is scared the first time, but getting the help that you need is the most important thing.

❧12❧

Personal Experiences of Anxiety

We feel really honoured that the following people (Josh, Emmeline, Scott, Bobbi, Leon and Phoebe) have shared their stories with us for this book.

The following stories are from young people (and slightly older people looking back) who have struggled with their anxiety, and found ways to cope with it. Some names and ages have been changed to keep them confidential.

Josh – age 27

I've always been an anxious person. For as long as I can remember, and still now, I worry that what I do isn't good enough or that everyone is expecting more from me. In my head, at school, I'd torment myself that if I wasn't the best, and didn't produce my best, that I'd be letting myself and loved ones down. The sweaty palms, that horrible knot in the pit of my stomach and the little voice in the back of my head, were reminders of the impending wave of anxiety that made it feel like it was easier to withdraw and not give the best of myself than it was to fail.

Ironic really, that the line of work I went into would mean trying to perform on a pitch in front of thousands of people, and at times intensify those feelings to such a point where I felt paralysed and wondered whether it was worth carrying on. This over-thinking, and the subsequent guilt that I felt from not enjoying this unbelievably fortunate position I found myself in, only made those feelings worse. For a long time, I had toyed with the idea of speaking to someone about how I felt, to get help to cope. I had always brushed it off as me being soft and these feelings being something I just needed to deal with myself. This all came to a head after a game in which I remember vividly everything I did seemed to be the wrong option. I was taking the path of least resistance in every decision I made and hated myself for it. It was then that I decided enough was enough and through a friend I found Ben [psychologist].

For me, I realised at this point, being able to share my anxieties, worries and concerns and to talk them through felt like the weight of the world had been lifted off my shoulders. Together we discussed different techniques and formulated tangible goals as focal points to move forward.

Mindfulness and the breathing techniques associated with it were something I was always a bit sceptical about, but can now count them as a daily practice and something that has proved invaluable. It has helped me take control of my over-active, over-thinking mind. In games and situations where I feel stressed, this, alongside a physical trigger (clicking my fingers), brings me back from wandering down those mental paths of "what if".

What I've realised more than anything is that there is no point fighting anxiety. Unless you hide under a rock or shy away from the world, the situations that make you feel anxious will always be there. What you can do is learn to share your feelings of anxiety and find techniques that work for you and let you take back control.

Emmeline – age 29

I'd always really enjoyed school, but when I was around 11 I dealt with a string of cruel emotional bullying from my 'best friends' at the time and it was that which really kick-started my journey with anxiety. At its height, I would feel sick at the prospect of going to school in the morning, I could barely eat my breakfast and I'd often have to leave lessons to see the school nurse because I felt so ill – it was a horrible time. The idea that I would be unwell in public eventually bled over from school life into anxiety about feeling that way on trips out, especially with places like the cinema where I wouldn't be able to leave if I needed to. At the time, I had no idea that what I was experiencing was anxiety – it just felt like a simmering pool of dread about something I didn't think I could tell anyone about. After a couple of years, some good talks with my family, a really brilliant new group of friends and a mantra of telling myself, "I don't feel sick, I feel excited," I managed to find my way through the crux of it and left a lot of the physical symptoms of anxiety behind me.

When I grew older, I experienced my first panic attack and similarly to when I was little, I had no idea what was happening (with all the chest pain I thought I was having a heart attack or something!). That experience brought back a lot of those same feelings I had when I was younger: a fear of having a panic attack, nausea or indeed (as the chest pains led me to believe something was seriously wrong) some kind of catastrophic emergency in public. It was only then, and with a little research, that it really clicked: I had been dealing with anxiety all along. Suddenly, the physical symptoms I'd been worried about made sense; and as much as I was reassured by that, knowing that anxiety was the cause AND result of these physical feelings didn't make them go away. I did a lot of research, I started meditating, I talked to people about what I was going through … but I couldn't quite shake that bundle of static and dread in my stomach; especially in places where if I did have a panic attack I'd feel stuck or judged by people around me. It kind of became the era of the back-up plan, or at least the era of preferring to stay in and watch Netflix, and I took stock of the fact it was negatively impacting my life – my own thoughts were sabotaging my happiness.

It was around this time that I experimented with using anxiety-calming apps on my phone, and one of them had a breath timer that repeated a green light for five seconds of breathing in, then a red light for 11 seconds of breathing out. I realised that using that (even if 11 seconds of breathing out seemed like ages!) really helped me bring myself back from the verge of panic; controlling my breath slowed my heart rate, relaxed my muscles and gave me a bit of space to focus on something other than hectic thoughts. Knowing I had my own secret hack to unpick my anxiety empowered me, and I began just saying yes to opportunities that came my way – "Yes, I will go to that party!" "Yes, I will go into the city on my own!" "Yes, I will do that presentation in front of 60 students!" It was tough, but the more I took the opportunities and realised that (a) I could get through them (or even enjoy them!) without incident and (b) even If anything happened, people are usually so caught up in their own issues that it wouldn't matter, the more confident I became. The big challenge came when I booked myself in to be an extra in a Hollywood film – seriously! – it was nerve-wracking, but I rekindled those thoughts of "This isn't fear, it's excitement" and I ended up having an amazing five hours of filming. Now, I can look back on that, and on all of my experiences with anxiety to date, and think, "If I can get through that, I can do anything" and since then, even if I feel hesitant, I've refused to let my anxiety stop me from taking a chance on an exciting opportunity.

Scott – age 16

I have recently been through a few major changes in my life which caused me to feel anxious. I moved house and high school at the beginning of Year 10, just at the start of my GCSE period. This caused me to feel very anxious because I am a very withdrawn person; I didn't know anyone and the idea of talking to people really scared me. Since I could be seen as nerdy, there is a lot of stigma attached that nerds are quite snobby. I would want to talk to a person; however I didn't want to say anything stupid or find out that they didn't like me. So, I constantly wished that someone would talk to me first, so that that way I wasn't as much to blame. However this rarely happened, and since I wasn't used to socialising, when it did happen I didn't really know what to do.

I started to become less anxious when a group of people accepted me into their group. They told me that loads of people wanted to talk to me; however I always seemed like I didn't want to be talked to, so I asked them why I appeared that way. They were all very nice and told me that I just seemed so nervous whenever anyone else was near, and said that I should just try and chill out.

Though this was difficult, I now had a group of friends who I knew wouldn't be mean to me, so I started getting comfortable around them. Getting those few friends really helped boost my self-confidence whenever they were around, so I started acting more like myself around them. Because of this, other people would see me with this group and I no longer felt like I had to hide myself from those around me. Due to this, I slowly started to feel a bit more comfortable around everyone around me, and I was no longer as reclusive as I used to be.

The second major change was going to college. Though I had a couple of friends coming to my college, a few others lost contact all of a sudden and I found it very hard to get comfortable around the new people. For the first couple of weeks I didn't meet anyone new or really talk to anyone, quite simply because I was unfamiliar with my surroundings. I then started talking to people on my table in my subjects, as I felt like this could be done without them judging me. I started off talking about the subject, and why it interests them, and then the conversation would slowly become more casual. It was a slow process; however, I already feel more comfortable just because the people in my classes know who I really am so I no longer need to hide behind a charade of silence.

Though I don't like my anxiety being there, it has helped me in many ways too. Since I'm quite introverted, I can usually find time to get any work done and I have learned to enjoy my own company. It still comes back when I try and talk to people; however I have learned to mostly control it.

Bobbi – age 17

Anxiety. To a lot of people, this is just another word in the arsenal but, for someone living with it, such as myself, it is so much more. On a good day, it's like a shadow that threatens to swallow me; on a bad day, I can feel nothing else. Even to this day, the memory of what the pure fear felt like sticks with me. Every cliché I'd ever read about anxiety became a reality. My palms were sweaty, my mouth dried up and my stomach suddenly turned to lead. For me, panic attacks became a daily occurrence. They would come and they would go and every time they'd take a bit of my hope with them. Every minute of every day was torture. I was constantly anxious to the point of hating myself and my life and nothing I did would make the feelings go away. The only respite that I got was the 30 seconds between waking up and regaining consciousness.

Throughout my life, the object of my anxious thoughts has varied with the situations that I'm in at the time. When I was little, being away from my family was one of the main causes of feeling nervous. This changed as I grew up: from being worried about being in a fire, to dreading travelling, to fearing exams – as well as a whole host of other things. The point is that, due to the way I'm wired, anxiety is inevitable. It became apparent to me very quickly that ridding myself of the illness was never going to happen.

However, I also learnt that what I fear the most is fear itself. When every cliché about anxiety becomes a reality, you start to realise that the side effects of fear are often worse than the situation you find yourself in.

About six months later, I couldn't take it anymore and I broke down, confessing everything to my mum. The relief that I felt was unparalleled and I believed that I could begin living again. However, this was only the start of my journey. The pattern continued for years – literally my entire life. I thought that I would never get to feel normal. Eventually, I had a full-blown mental breakdown but, because of this, I finally got the help I needed. It took months of therapy and practice – I literally had to learn to think again. Now, for the first time in my whole life, I can finally live. I mean, really live, not just exist. Even though I still sometimes take dips, I know that I can come out of it and that is the difference between then and now. Before, I was just anxiety but now I am living, even if anxiety is sometimes present. Instead of letting my anxiety control me, I choose to control it. I have been given the knowledge of how to rationalise my thoughts and over time this has become my key back to reality. I'll admit that it was a lot harder than that sentence would suggest but, every day, things would get a little bit better – sometimes worse – but, overall, better.

For the first time in my life, I feel as though I have the skills to enjoy life. The fact that I have had to work for it makes it feel even sweeter, like the best prize anyone could get. So, it's true, happiness and a life without anxiety isn't easy. It is years of suffering followed by months of work. Getting better is probably one of the hardest choices that I ever had to make because I literally had to learn to think again. However, it is also the best choice I have ever made and I would not change it for anything.

Leon – age 12

Two years ago, I started high school, which was a massive change from primary school. My primary school was small and safe, but high school was big and frightening and it was quite easy to feel lost and forgotten about. It was scary in my first few days. I kept myself to myself at first, as this was much easier. I got pushed into making friends, as there were two other people standing on their own and a teacher got us to talk to each other. I had made two friends initially – one who was in my form class, Jack, and another who was in a form in the other half of the school, Ian.

At first, I thought high school was OK. I wasn't one of the "popular" kids but I was all right with that. However, it didn't take long for some of those "popular" kids to start making fun of me. They would call me names in and outside the classroom, follow me down the corridor at break times. People stole my tie. Others would pull at my coat or my bag causing damage to my uniform. I didn't like it and I would tell them to stop but it made no difference. It made me feel really sad and unhappy and I didn't understand what I had done to them to make them so horrible to me.

School felt like an unsafe place to be as people were picking on me 24/7. After a while, I realised that ignoring them wouldn't work so I just tried to forget about it. However, it just got worse and it started to affect my schoolwork and my behaviour. People were making me scared and angry, but I didn't want to show it at school because I didn't want them to have anything else to pick on. I was bottling it all up and I felt like a living bomb ready to explode. I just didn't want to be at school. I was different from other people and felt like nobody liked me, nobody wanted to be my friend and everything was my fault. I just wanted to hide. I didn't want to go to school, but I knew that I had to.

Then it started to affect my home life too. Teachers would ring my parents complaining of my behaviour. I would also come home and argue with my mum, dad and brother because I had bottled everything up at school and all my upset, worry and anger just needed to come out. I stole things to give to people in the hope that they would like me but it didn't work. As a consequence, my mum and dad would ground me so I would spend even more time on my own. I felt so lonely, that the whole world was against me and that I had no one on my side fighting my corner.

Eventually my mum contacted the headmaster for some help because she believed that my behaviour at home was linked to school life somehow. The head of year met with me and my mum and they put a plan in place to make school feel like it was a safer place.

It was coming to the end of my first high school year and my mum asked if I could be moved form groups to the other half of the school. It gave me an opportunity to start fresh. A new year, a new form class, new teachers and new kids. I soon met a group of friends who were like me in a kind of way; a group with whom I could be myself and they accepted me for who I am.

Later that year, my head of year invited me to be part of the Diana Award Anti-Bullying Campaign. I was so happy to be asked that I jumped at the chance. I went on a training day and learnt lots of things about bullying and what can be done to prevent it. I am now an anti-bullying ambassador and help others who are feeling the way I used to and share with them the actions that I took to help address the challenges that I faced at school.

Now that I have my head of year on my side, parents who understand the problems I've had, friends who accept me for who I am, and the opportunity to prevent bullying happening to other kids, I am in a much happier place at school right now and ready to take on my GCSEs. I would advise anyone going through what I did to tell someone, an adult or a friend that you trust, so they can help you get through whatever your problem is.

Phoebe – age 18

I was always described as an 'anxious child' and referred to as 'too sensitive'. As I grew older and entered my teenage years, what everyone always thought was something I'd grow out of, became much bigger and harder to handle. When I was 11, my anxiety began to snowball. I would get incredibly upset over not completing schoolwork to the 'best of my ability' or receiving a lower grade than I thought I should and I dreaded going to school and interacting with my classmates. From here, I began to express my anxiety through obsessions and compulsions which was the start of a battle with rituals and obsessive thinking that would later take over my life.

Throughout high school, my worries grew and grew. I would worry about losing friends, about missing homework, about something happening to my family and about being what I deemed 'a failure', amongst a multitude of other things. Some of my worries were understandable to others but some of them were dubbed 'irrational' and I grew shameful of my anxiety.

When I was in Year 10, I began to experience panic attacks. They became so bad that I couldn't sit in a class for the full duration of a lesson without having to run out. My legs would shake under the table and I would become sweaty, shaky and scared. I would feel as though I couldn't breathe and panicked that something was happening to me. I worried that I would never be able to breathe properly again and sometimes it even felt as though I might die or at least pass out. Sometimes there wasn't any specific reason for this to happen but I couldn't control it. For a while, there wasn't a day that passed when I didn't experience a panic attack.

Aged 15, I entered mental health services and eventually started CBT with an amazing therapist who helped me tackle my problems head on. I addressed the ever-growing list of rituals that had taken over my life and looked at my anxiety from a completely new standpoint. I filled out sheets and worked through a lot of the reasons why I had developed such problematic anxiety, ranging from how I thought about things to difficult experiences in my past. A lot of the work was very difficult and it took a while but I eventually got there. Aged 18, I was discharged from services and began to reclaim my life and work towards my goals.

I am in a much better place now and have achieved feats I never thought were possible. I have developed methods of coping with my anxiety and have completely got rid of some of my symptoms. My anxiety is still an issue and it is something I consciously work on every day but I never dreamt that I would be living the life I am currently living.

One of the main symptoms of my anxiety was avoidance. I would go to ridiculous lengths to avoid situations and feelings. This hindered my recovery and made it take longer. Committing to recovery is one of the hardest things I ever did but I cannot emphasise enough the benefits I have felt from that decision. I never thought I would be able to get public transport without freaking out or attend school or college again. I never thought I'd be able to stay away from home for periods of time or get a job. But I have achieved all of these things. Right now, I am the best I have been for many years. I have a job that I love and I am looking to re-start sixth form and pursue my dream of attending university. I am planning for my future and although I still have anxiety, I have learnt ways to control it and lessen it. Recovery *is* possible. I used to believe it wasn't possible, at least not for me, but I now realise just how wrong I was. Recovery is possible for everyone, including you.

❧ 13 ❧

My Anxiety
Survival Plan

In this chapter, we are going to put together an "Anxiety Survival Plan" which can include information you have collected from the other chapters. The idea is to create an understanding of your own individual anxiety, and think about what can help you to feel more in control of it.

My Anxiety Is...

(Maybe draw a picture or write words.) What would I call it (anxiety/worry/noise)? What shape is it? Colour? Is it a person or an object?

What Can Make Me Vulnerable To Anxiety...

Lack of sleep? Transition or change coming up? Meeting new people/new situations? Lots of difficult things happening at the same time? Studying too much – working too hard?

My Anxious Bodily Reactions...

What do I notice in my body (e.g. breathing speeding up, butterflies in stomach)? (See Chapter 1 for ideas.)

My Anxious Thoughts...

What thoughts tend to pop into my head? (See Chapter 4 for information on "catching thoughts".) What shortcuts or errors are most likely to catch me out?

My Anxious Behaviours...

What do I tend to do when I'm anxious (e.g. avoiding things, withdrawing, getting cross with myself or others)?

My Triggers...

What kind of situations or things lead to me feeling anxious or worried (e.g. exams, arguments with friends, spiders)?

Times/Places When I Am More Likely To Be Anxious Are...

Am I more likely to be anxious in the morning or evening, day or night, or at weekends? Are there particular times when I will be more anxious such as before an exam? Are there places I am more likely to be anxious such as crowded places where I don't know anyone? At home, school or when I'm out and about? Particular dates or times of the year?

Who I Can Talk To About My Anxiety...

Who are the best people to talk to about my anxiety who can support me through it?

How I Can Let Them Know/What I Can Say If I'm Struggling...

(See Chapter 11 for ideas.)

What I Can Do If My Anxiety Is Feeling Overwhelming...

Think about the skills that I have learned in Chapters 3, 4, 5, 6 and 7, and any more coping strategies that I might have. Thought challenging? Selfsoothing? Mindfulness? (Be as specific about strategies as possible.)

How I Can Help My Body To Feel Calmer...

(See Chapter 7 for examples of strategies.)

How I Can Deal With My Anxious Thoughts...

(See Chapter 6 for examples of mindfulness strategies, or Chapter 4 for thought challenging.) What alternative, more helpful thoughts (or mantras, or positive coping statements) could I use instead?

Things I Can Do To Reduce My Anxiety...

Is there anything else I can do that helps me to quickly reduce my anxiety?

Who Else Is There To Support Me...

Friend? Family member or carer? Teacher? Helpline? Other trusted person?

What Other People Can Do...

What can other people do that feels helpful when I am anxious? For example, stay with me, give me a hug, buy me some ice-cream, remind me to use my strategies, practise slowing down breathing with me.

It might be useful to look through this plan (and have copies of it if you need to) when you are starting to feel anxious. You might also want to share it with someone close to you, to help them to learn more about your anxiety and know how best to support you. You might also want to share it with school or college. If you let people know when you are struggling, then they can help you to get back on track and you don't have to do it alone.

Useful Information

Helplines

Contact Childline on 0800 11111 or via website:
www.childline.org.uk/get-support

Call the Samaritans on 116 123, email jo@samaritans.org
or use the Next Generation Text Service (for people who
are hard of hearing) – information available on website:
www.samaritans.org

Further information about anxiety

YoungMinds: www.youngminds.org.uk/find-help/
conditions/anxiety

Anxiety UK: https://www.anxietyuk.org.uk/our-services/
anxiety-information/young-people-and-anxiety

HeadMeds (information about medication):
www.headmeds.org.uk/conditions/6-anxiety

Book for parents

Cartwright-Hatton, S. (2007) *Coping with an Anxious or Depressed Child: A CBT Guide for Parents*. London: Oneworld.

Information about school/exam stress

NSPCC guidance leaflet 'Beat Exam Stress': available for download at: www.nspcc.org.uk

Pomodoro Technique: see www.pomodorotechnique.com

Student Minds (the UK's Student Mental Health Charity): visit www.studentminds.org.uk or info@studentminds.org.uk

YoungMinds 'School Stress Campaign Pack'

BIBLIOGRAPHY

(Please also see the Useful Information section.)

Barnes, C.M. and Drake, C.L. (2015) 'Prioritizing sleep health: Public health policy recommendations.' *Perspectives on Psychological Science, 10, 6, 733–737.*

Cartwright-Hatton, S., Roberts, C., Chitsabesan, P., Fothergill, C. and Harrington, R. (2004) 'Systematic review of the efficacy of cognitive behaviour therapies for childhood and adolescent anxiety disorders.' *British Journal of Clinical Psychology, 43, 4, 421–436.*

Chaskalson, M. (2014) *Mindfulness in Eight Weeks.* London: Harper Thorsons.

Coan, J.A., Schaefer, H.S. and Davidson, R.J. (2006) 'Lending a hand: Social regulation of the neural response to threat.' *Psychological Medicine, 17, 12, 1032–9.*

Costello, E.J., Copeland, W. and Angold, A. (2011) 'Trends in psychopathology across the adolescent years: What changes when children become adolescents, and when adolescents become adults?' *The Journal of Child Psychology and Psychiatry, 52, 10, 1015–1025.*

Fox, N.A., Henderson, H.A., Marshall, P.J., Nichols, K.E. and Ghera, M.M. (2005) 'Behavioral inhibition: Linking biology and behavior within a developmental framework.' *Annual Review of Psychology, 56, 1, 235–262.*

Gerhardt, S. (2004) *Why Love Matters.* Hove: Brunner Routledge.

Hirshkowitz, M., Whiton, K., Albert, S.M., Alessi, C. *et al.* (2015) 'National Sleep Foundation's sleep time duration recommendations: Methodology and results summary.' *Sleep Health, 1,* 1, 40–43.

Hoffman, S.G. (2008) 'Cognitive processes during fear acquisition and extinction in animals and humans: Implications for exposure therapy of anxiety disorders.' *Clinical Psychology Review, 28,* 2, 199–210.

Kahneman, D. (2011) *Thinking, Fast and Slow.* New York: Farrar Straus and Giroux.

Kessler, R.C., Angermeyer, M., Anthony, J.C., De Graaf, R. *et al.* (2007) 'Lifetime prevalence and age-of-onset distributions of mental disorders in the World Health Organization's World Mental Health Survey Initiative.' *World Psychiatry, 6,* 3, 168–176.

Polanczyk, G.V., Salum, G.A., Sugaya, L.S., Caye, A. and Rohde, L.A. (2015) 'Annual Research Review: A meta-analysis of the worldwide prevalence of mental disorders in children and adolescents.' *Journal of Child Psychology and Psychiatry, 56,* 3, 1–21.

Rutter, M., Kim-Cohen, J. and Maughan, B. (2006) 'Continuities and discontinuities in psychopathology between childhood and adult life.' *The Journal of Child Psychology and Psychiatry, 47,* 3–4, 276–295.

Stewart, R.E. and Chambless, D.L. (2009) 'Cognitive-behavioral therapy for adult anxiety disorders in clinical practice: A meta-analysis of effectiveness studies.' *Journal of Consulting and Clinical Psychology, 77,* 4, 595–606.

Williams, M. and Penman, D. (2011) *Mindfulness: A Practical Guide to Finding Peace in a Frantic World.* London: Piatkus.

Yoost, B.L. and Crawford, L.R. (2015) *Fundamentals of Nursing: Active Learning for Collaborative Practice.* Missouri: Elsevier.

INDEX